Fatal Crossing

A Novella

The Poppy McGowan Mysteries
Book 3

Pamela Hart

Chapter 1

November

I know it's wrong to be glad about a not-for-profit organisation being broke. Especially the Australian Institute of Archaeology in Jordan, the place my boyfriend, Tol, was supposed to be working. But, since a grant had been delayed, it now couldn't afford to pay him for three months, rather than the six weeks they'd originally said.

I felt guilty about being happy, but I was very, very happy. I was trying to hide it, because a supportive person would not be happy about their significant other's professional disaster. But I'm not good at hiding things, especially from Tol.

Rather sweetly, he was pretending to be happy, too.

At dinner on a Thursday with me and Annie, who is both my friend and his boss, he graciously accepted a two-month contract with the Museum of NSW.

'Wonderful!' he said, toying with the sugar spoon. I've learnt to keep my eyes on Tol's hands when I want to know how he's feeling. Those long pianist's fingers are very revealing. Toying with the sugar spoon was a sign of moderate stress. He smiled bravely. 'I'll be able to really get to grips with that Indigenous collection from Bourke and get it in a state to be exhibited.'

Poor baby.

Annie grinned at him. 'Never mind, possum, the grant will come through soon.'

Tol grinned back, his hazel eyes crinkling with genuine amusement. 'At least I get to spend more time with you, Annie.'

'Oh, yeah, like it's me you want to spend time with,' she retorted, flicking a glance at me. I smiled, trying not to look like the cat with the cream.

'*That*,' Tol said, taking my hand and kissing it, 'is the one truly good thing about all this.'

Sigh.

We were having a celebratory dinner because the next day I was moving into my freshly renovated house in Annandale. My tiny, gorgeous little house which I had spent seven months restoring to its Victorian origins (except the bathroom, because I ran out of money, but at least the plumbing worked). After seven months of living with my parents, I was looking forward to my own home again.

Not to mention having privacy to share with Tol.

———

'I TOLD HER, "I can't give you money I don't bloody have," but she doesn't believe me. Centrelink's told her, the Child Support Agency's told her, but she *still* thinks I'm doin' her down.'

Maybe because you lied to her all through your marriage and had bits on the side, I thought, having heard the first installment of the removal man's life history at the self-storage depot where they'd picked up my furniture. I didn't say anything. I've learnt not to—nodding is all they need, the people who tell me their life story. It happens all the time. People just tell me stuff. God knows why. I don't encourage them. I hardly ever even ask questions.

'Careful with that bookcase,' I said. 'It's got glass doors.'

He nodded and eased my lovely little leadlighted 1930's book-case off the truck into the waiting arms of his offsider, then continued without a breath, 'So I said, "Come over to my house and f-I mean, bloody look for yourself." I live like one of those old monk blokes. I've got nuffin. But she wouldn't do that. Oh, no. Might have to shut up and stop complainin'.'

My sympathies were all with the woman. He might live simply, but he had the latest iPhone and was wearing some very expensive Nike trainers. Cravenly, I didn't point this out. Because I wanted my bookcase to reach my lounge room in one piece.

As I work in television and have rather erratic hours, I can get days off in lieu of overtime, so we were moving on a Friday when the removalists were cheaper. Tol took the day off to help, God bless him, and the non-working part of my family were much in evidence, carting my plants and clothes over from my parents' house a few blocks away, making cups of tea, and telling the removal men to put the furniture in exactly the places I didn't want it.

The third time Aunty Mary insisted, 'The couch would be much better under that little window,' I said meaningfully, 'I think it's getting a bit crowded in here, don't you Mum?', and my mother smiled at me and shepherded Mary and Dad back to their house for lunch.

Tol slung an arm around my shoulders and hugged. 'Your aunty is a force of nature,' he said.

'A tsunami.'

I leant my head back against him and watched the now blessedly silent removal men position the couch in the middle of the room, where it formed a room divider from the dining area.

My house was once a basic worker's cottage. Originally, you walked straight into a small parlour, then down a corridor on the right. A door half-way down the corridor led left into the only bedroom. Down a step at the end of the corridor into the kitchen. In the 1920s they had added a bathroom/laundry beyond the kitchen. In the '50s or '60s, they had joined the laundry to the outside toilet so you could go to the dunny from the inside.

The woman who owned it before me had put on an upper storey with two small bedrooms and knocked out the wall between the parlour and bedroom to make an L-shaped room. The corridor was still there. I'd wanted to remove it, but apparently it was holding up the roof.

So I was using the old bedroom area for dining, and the parlour as my lounge room. Did I mention the whole house is only 12 feet wide? I'd had to cull a lot of furniture, but it was worth it. I looked around: cheerful yellow walls, beautiful plaster work, ceiling roses and rose-patterned cornices, shining wooden floors... I was very happy.

My phone rang. It was Tyler, the head of News and Current Affairs at the ABC, where I work in the children's department.

'Oh, god,' I groaned. 'What does he want? Hello, Tyler.'

'Are you sure you don't want to work for me, sweetheart?'

What, I thought, work for a patronising man in a polo shirt who kept calling me sweetheart even though I'd asked him not to? Work in the incredibly stressful world of current affairs instead of the fun and friendly world of children's TV?

'No, thank you, Tyler.'

'Last chance. I've got to appoint someone for the *Daily Report* researcher's position today.'

'No, thank you.'

'Your loss.' He hung up, sounding grumpy. Too bad. Tyler had trouble believing that anyone could *not* want to work in NewsCaff.

'A lot of people would kill for that job,' Tol observed.

'A lot of people would kill for *my* job.'

In fact, I thought, as I looked around my slowly filling home, a lot of people would kill for my life. Great man, fun job, lovely little house, nice family. I smiled up at Tol, a bit misty, and he kissed me. Oh, yes, great man who's a great kisser.

After the removalists had gone, we didn't bother to put sheets on the bed before we christened it.

———

THE NEXT FEW weeks were some of the best of my life. Work was steady and enjoyable, Tol and I spent as much time together as possible, and I unpacked and sorted and culled and arranged until my little house was just right. I revelled in my regained independence. I didn't have to tell anyone if I was going to be out late, or not home for dinner. It was like the heady rush of leaving home during University days, but better because I wasn't living in a fairly squalid one-bedroom flat with Annie where we had to survive on a diet of home made chicken soup and meat my father donated (he was a meat inspector). No, now I had a lovely house and Tol for company and we ate very well indeed because now I had my own kitchen back (however basic) I engaged in a frenzy of cooking.

The only sour note was having to testify at the committal hearing of the step-daughter and grandson of a friend of Aunty Mary's who had tried to murder her (the friend, that is). Horrible. But that was only one day, and Tol was with me because he was a witness too.

That night, a Friday, I expunged the court demons with osso bucco followed by a pavlova. Tol finished his second helping of dessert and sat back with a sigh and the glazed eyes of a sugar rush.

'I had no idea you were this domestic,' he said.

'Is that bad?' I wondered if he was disappointed. You know, you think your girlfriend's this go-getting career woman and she turns out to be Martha Stewart instead. (Though I don't see why I can't be both. Only Nigella Lawson instead of Martha Stewart.)

'Bad? No! It's great. The only thing I don't like about living on my own is cooking.'

That sentence was both very good and very bad, I thought, so I rushed into speech to cover my reaction.

'I don't like washing up.'

'I'd rather wash up than cook. Deal?'

'Deal.' I felt warmth spread out from my solar plexus and infuse my whole body. That sounded like a long-term deal to me, and it felt like it, too. I went around the table, sat on Tol's lap and bent to kiss him—and my phone rang.

'Bugger it.'

Reluctantly, I got up and fished it out of my bag.

Tyler again. I gritted my teeth.

'Hello, Tyler.'

'You've got to help me out, Poppy.' Poppy? He *never* called me by my name.

'What's the problem?'

'That researcher I hired—that Jane girl—she's been killed in a car accident. I need you in her chair Monday.'

'That's terrible!'

'Yes, yes, it's terrible.' His voice slowed and calmed a little as he contemplated the truth behind his crisis, but News people are used to dealing with horrible events, and he forged on. 'But I'm down one researcher already with flu and another's going off on long service leave in two weeks and I need you in that chair *immediately*.'

'But-'

'It's not permanent. Just for a month, to tide us over until we can find replacements. '

Oh. Ok, I could probably cope with NewsCaff for a month, and my work at *Launchpad*, the junior tv series I worked on, wasn't at a critical point. But there was still one major obstacle.

'Jennifer Jay-' I began. My producer, Jennifer Jay, used to have Tyler's job, and she frowned mightily on him trying to poach me.

'I've spoken to Jennifer Jay,' Tyler interrupted me, ' and she's agreed to second you for a month. And not a day more.'

I could hear her say it.

'Well, if it's only a month...'

'Nine o'clock Monday. I'll see you then,' he said, and hung up. I hate the way people have stopped saying goodbye. It really pisses me off. In fact, I was thoroughly pissed off. I rang Tyler straight back.

'Yes?' he snapped.

'I haven't said "yes" yet, Tyler,' I said, sweet as pie.

There was a silence at the other end.

'What do you want, McGowan?' he growled finally.

'What are you offering?'

'I can't pay you more than the others are getting. You know how that works.' I did. At the ABC, pay scales were fixed and there were no sweeteners. I thought for a nanosecond. There *was* something I wanted, and Tyler could organise it.

'I want a ride in the helicopter.'

Another silence.

'Done. Nine o'clock Monday.'

And he hung up.

Tol was looking at me with that mixture of amusement and affection which always turned my heart over.

'You are a clever little thing, aren't you?' he said.

'It's bad for Tyler to get everything he wants without paying for it,' I said, tilting my nose in the air like Mary Poppins. I sat back down in his lap again. 'And I've *always* wanted to go up in a helicopter!'

Chapter 2

Monday

So at nine o'clock on Monday morning, I plunged into a messy, high-pressured and not at all creative world as the new researcher for the *Daily Report*, a half-hour national current affairs program that aired weekdays just after the main news bulletin.

The host, Carol Stanhope, had moved up the ranks as a reporter and had the reputation of being cruel but fair as an interviewer. Tyler was my ultimate boss, but my immediate boss was Barry Woods, a tubby, grey haired, fidgety man whose main aim in life was to wipe the nose of News by getting scoops first and making News play snippets of *Daily's* interviews on the main News broadcast.

Which was partly my job, and partly the job of the reporters, of whom there were two in Sydney, where the office was, one in Canberra, and four in the other capital cities. They doubled as News reporters too, which led to some timetabling tussles with the News desks in those cities. Overseas stories were handled either by ABC foreign correspondents, shared by all NewsCaff, or by stringers (freelance journalists who worked regularly for us) brought on for an individual stories.

All of this I already knew as I walked in. I had also known enough to read every metropolitan daily online over breakfast, and to at least glance at *The Times, The Washington Post,* and *The New York Tribune.*

The ABC, thank God, doesn't do celebrity gossip, so I didn't have to delve into the tabloids.

Barry, alone in the office, greeted me with a lot of thankfulness and a little wariness. Fair enough. It wasn't like I was a veteran news researcher. I had a few butterflies of my own about whether I could handle this. But I have learnt that employers usually know if you can handle a job. Often I've been asked to do jobs which I wasn't qualified for (frankly, that's how I got the *Launchpad* job, off the back of some technical writing I did for the children's department) but I've taken them on and it's been fine. I'd told myself that a lot over the weekend.

'We've put you on the soft stuff for now,' Barry said reassuringly. Soft stuff = human interest stories, not hard news. He handed me a file marked *Playgrounds*. 'Jane was researching a story on how children's playgrounds have changed over the years and how safety considerations have removed a lot of the equipment kids used to love.'

'Like merry-go-rounds,' I said immediately. He looked blank. 'You know, those things that spin and you push them and jump on and the centrifugal force tries to push you off...'

'Carousels. Yes. That was one of the things Jane mentioned. And covering up the chains on swings and no wooden seats anymore so you can't stand up to swing.'

I nodded. All this was familiar to me from taking my nieces and nephews to the park.

'She's made a list of playgrounds we could film at,' he said. 'We need you to do a recce.' Suddenly he looked embarrassed. 'Um... we were going to can the story, but Jane was very keen on it so we thought we should, um, do it in, um, honour of her.'

I must have looked puzzled, because his gaze sharpened on me. 'She was doing this recce when she had the accident,' he explained. 'Went off a bridge into Galston Gorge. She'd found some old playground out there that hasn't been touched since the '60s and thought we could get some 'before' shots there, you know?'

He tapped the file. 'It's on the list. But the bridge is being repaired, so you'll have to go around the long way. And you'll need a car from the pool.'

I nodded, astounded and very slightly admiring at the professionalism (ruthlessness?) which sent an employee out alone on the same errand that had killed her predecessor.

But at least I knew what I was doing. Recces I could do—I did them all the time for *Launchpad*. Recce (pronounced recky) is short for reconnaissance, a piece of World War II slang (via the French Resistance) for checking out enemy territory.

I rang the car pool and organised a car, and read through Jane's notes. They were admirably clear and readable. I tried to ignore the loopy handwriting and the little circles over the top of the 'i's. I was sure that Jane had only recently stopped putting smiley faces in them, and that saddened me.

I stopped by Barry's desk to sign the in/out sheet. A few spaces above my name, the loopy handwriting spelled out 'Jane

Mancus'.

'She was a Mancus?' I asked Barry, surprised. The Mancuses are big players in Sydney—rich, political, social, philanthropic. They made their money using virtual slave labour in the sugar fields of Queensland in the 19th century, but no one mentions that now.

'A poor cousin,' Barry said.

'How old was she?'

Remembering those empty smiley faces, I expected him to say '20', or '25' at the oldest, but he frowned, estimated, and said, 'Forty? Around that, I think. She'd been in our offices in Orange.'

Orange is a big country town in NSW. They grow apples there. In that context, 'our' meant the ABC, not NewsCaff.

A country girl. Maybe that explained how a forty year old woman still felt the world deserved smiley faces?

I felt sorry that we'd never met.

I tackled the inner city playgrounds before I took on the long drive to Galston Gorge.

I was in Newtown, hiding from the late summer heat under the soaring shade sails, watching a gaggle of kids playing, jumping, digging, sliding and giggling, and thinking that modern playgrounds were actually a big improvement for the very little kids, even if they were blander, when my phone rang.

It was Detective Inspector Chloe Prudhomme, the lead detective on that murder case. Bugger. We'd already testified. What else did we have to do?

'Hello, Detective Inspector,' I said.

'Ms McGowan,' she acknowledged. That's about all you get from her in the way of 'hellos'. 'What do you know about the News and Current Affairs department?'

'I'm sorry?'

'Can you-' She hesitated. '- can you give me some background information on the News and Current Affairs Department?'

'I've just started there today!' I protested. 'Besides, why do you want to know?' I grinned. 'Has Tyler been cooking the books?'

'That would be Fraud. We're Major Crimes. And *I'm* a homicide detective, as you very well know.'

Oh yes, I knew. To my cost. But no one was dead. Except—

'Jane was *murdered*?'

'We're treating the death as suspicious,' Detective Chloe said repressively, but that didn't mean anything. As she'd implied, Chloe didn't get wheeled out for anything less serious than murder.

I felt wildly thankful that I hadn't known Jane, after all. I'd known two other women who were murdered, and it was horrible. Really heart-breaking.

'That's horrible,' I said.

Chloe relented a little.

'It might be suicide, or even accidental death,' she said. 'I've just been pulled in because it's a Mancus and the Force has to be seen to be doing its best. We're waiting for the autopsy report. But we know she was drunk at the very least, and maybe drugs were involved.'

I sighed with relief. Suicide was marginally better. At least I didn't have to look sideways at my co-workers. Accident would be best.

'So why do you want to know about NewsCaff?'

'Standard procedure. Investigate the victim's associates and environments.'

'So why not just interview everyone there?'

'The ABC is closing ranks, and the Mancuses are backing it. I can't get anywhere—you know I can't *force* people to be interviewed unless I arrest them.'

That was true. And I could imagine the Mancus family would have a lot of pull.

'You said you'd just started there today,' Chloe prompted. 'Does that mean you're actually *in* the department?'

'I'm seconded until they find a replacement for Jane.'

'Excellent.' The satisfaction was fat in her voice, and that irked me.

'I've had enough of death and investigations. Don't pull me into this.'

'I don't need you to spy, but I need background. I need to understand how these people operate. If it's suicide, I need to make sure it was unprompted.'

'Well, that's easy enough. Tyler will give that to you. You can get her notes.'

'Not without a subpoena,' Chloe said grimly. 'The ABC is citing the journalists' right to protect a source—a right I'm not at all sure covers researchers, let me tell you—and they're fighting it in court and refusing to let their people talk to us. I don't know why. Just so we don't set a precedent, I suspect. Tyler says he's prepared to go to gaol in defence of the principal and you can imagine the media storm that would generate. There's nothing in her apartment. We have to get at this information some other way.'

'I have her notes,' I said slowly. I wasn't sure I liked the way this was going. The ABC was right that sources should be protected; though Jane, as far as I knew, didn't *have* any sources. But Chloe was a good cop, and we should support good cops, right? My stomach was in knots, though. It was true—I had had enough of murder and investigation. I just wanted to enjoy my life after the upheavals of the last few months.

'You can make me copies.'

'No. That would mean I'd broken confidentiality.' I was sure I couldn't do that. 'But I can look through her notes and see if there's anything unusual.'

'How are you going to know what's unusual?'

'I'll have a better chance of spotting it than you will.'

There was a pause. I could picture Detective Chloe thinking, all medium brown hair and medium height and medium everything except intelligence and drive.

'All right. I'll call you tomorrow.'

She hung up. Another one who didn't say goodbye.

Curiously, I didn't mind being a last resort. It was endearing to think of Detective Chloe being at a loss.

I took the notes and the photos I needed, but I wondered what the hell Jane had been doing, planning to recce this site. I could have found out everything we needed on Google Earth.

So I went to one of Newtown's many excellent cafes with my laptop and checked out all the other sites on Jane's list. The only one which wasn't properly covered by Google Earth or a council website was the one out by the Gorge. The playground was over-shadowed by enormous trees and it wasn't owned by the council. Not nearly enough data to make decisions about a shoot.

I read through Jane's notes with extra attention, of course, but there was nothing in the whole folder which might interest Detective Chloe, except that the gushy style and the exclamation points might have given an insight into Jane's character. Occasionally she even forgot to be an adult and put in the smiley face. It didn't seem like the habit of someone given to suicide, but then, sometimes the happiest people could also crash the hardest. And maybe the smiley faces were a sign that she had been high rather than naïve.

I headed out full of curiosity about a dead woman. I would have to ask someone—not Barry. Gina Kirkidis, one of the reporters. She was with News, but she would have checked Jane out. I knew Gina and she would give me the good oil.

Before I went, I looked on the traffic alert site. They'd cleared the bridge that Jane had driven off. No doubt they'd worked through the weekend, because the Galston Gorge bridge was the only connection between Dural and Hornsby Heights, and was therefore the Dural residents' main access to the north. The two suburbs were separated by a national park, and the bridge crossed Berowra Creek at the bottom of—well, a gorge.

What I didn't understand was why Jane had been in the Gorge at all. According to Google maps—and, come to that, my own knowledge of Sydney—there weren't any houses, and certainly no playgrounds there. The address she had marked for visiting was an old Baptist church just outside Dural. It would have been much, much faster to go via West Pennant Hills than by the Gorge.

I reached the old church by 11.30, took two seconds to realise that the overgrown, badly maintained 'playground' was more a deathtrap than a trip down memory lane (which was why, the cleaning lady at the church told me, it had been fenced off with barbed wire). I was done here.

And that was when I cheated.

I happened to know, because of a *Launchpad* episode I had researched the year before, that there was a lovely contemporary sequence of kids playing in a '60s playground in the ABC archives, including hair-raising footage of a girl swinging so high while standing up on the swing that she is almost parallel to the ground.

It had taken me more than an hour and a half to find that footage in the first place. The ABC film archive is a wondrous place, but the millions of hours of footage were catalogued at the time they were shot, and this had merely been tagged: 'children at play'. There were 577 'children at play' entries in the database.

So if I were a *real* NewsCaff researcher, it would take me an hour and a half to find the footage they needed for their story, right? Which meant that if I took, say, an hour to drive down Galston Gorge and back to Ultimo the long way, then they were half an hour better off. Right?

What would you have done if you were me?

Chapter 3

Monday

The ABC car pool has two types of cars: little bitty ones for individuals, and big V8 station wagons or SUVs for camera crews. The *theory* is everyone gets what they need. In practice, if you ring up at 9.15 on a Monday morning and say you need a car, you get what's left over.

In my case, that was an old tank of a station wagon which was supposed to have power steering but which dragged at the wheel like a bullock team.

Not a problem on the fine roads of our fine metropolis, right? Right. I had made it up to Dural with only a few swear words. But as I turned onto Galston Road and left the suburbs behind, all that changed.

Normally, I'd have enjoyed the drive. If I'd been in my own car, I'd have loved it: the summer smell of the bush, all lemon myrtle and dry eucalyptus, the sun flickering through the tall gum trees, laying down filigrees of light on the bitumen, the bellbirds chiming and lorikeets whistling in the bottlebrush, the incessant buzz of cicadas which was the essential sound of summer...

All right, I quite enjoyed it even when wrestling with a recalcitrant tank. But the bridge was at the bottom of a *gorge*, and getting that car safely to the bottom was hard. It was all too easy to speed up without anticipating the sudden corners which let the road down in easy stages to the creek. At every corner the car fought the wheel, and I was sweating buckets by the time I approached the creek and the bridge.

Was this why Jane had crashed? She'd only been at Ultimo a few weeks—had she been given one of these behemoths to drive and just been outclassed?

I was, maybe, a little *too* cautious going down the hill. The locals behind me on the two-laned road certainly thought so. There was too much traffic coming the other way for them to overtake, and they tailgated me all the way, which didn't help my nerves.

There's no stopping place near the bridge itself, but there's a parking area not far up the other side of the gorge, for people who want to go bushwalking in the national park. I pulled into it with relief and watched the cars behind me pick up speed as I got out of their way. I understood their frustration, but was it really necessary to give me the finger as they passed?

God, I thought, *I sound like Aunty Mary.*

I parked and got out, hit by the sun as one is in summer in Sydney, the heat coming up from the asphalt in a solid block, the breeze a mere promise of survival.

I reached for my go-everywhere hat (crunched in the bottom of my laptop bag) and walked back down to the bridge.

It harked back to an earlier day, another century. Solid timber baulks in a kind of cradle design meant that no car could have gone off the middle.

The repair work was evident. New side rails, oddly, at the near approach. So Jane had been driving *from* Hornsby Heights to the Dural side, and had gone over before she got onto the bridge proper. You have to make a sharp turn onto the bridge and another off it. Jane had clearly failed to make the turn on.

Half-afraid of what I was going to see, I approached the new rail and looked over. A drop of six or seven metres, with an almost-dry creek bed at the bottom. Rocks. The dirt and mud at the side had been churned up, presumably by the boots of the rescuers. There was nothing left of the car except some broken glass.

I imagined the scene: the helmet lights, the tow trucks waiting to winch the car up, the red warning lights blinking on the road... and realised that I didn't know what time Jane had crashed. She'd been working. It was probably full daylight.

That made Detective Chloe's suspicions clear. Because although it was a tricky drive, it wasn't *dangerous*. The road was properly sealed and graded, the guard rails were strong, the curves well sign-posted.

Which made me wonder if Jane had been dead before she went over.

Chapter 4

Monday/Tuesday

On the way back to the ABC offices at Ultimo, I went over in my head all the other footage of playgrounds that I'd found for the same program on play. I doubted we'd need to shoot any new footage. Which again made me wonder why the hell Jane had done the recce in the first place?

I'd taken Barry's instructions without thinking this morning because I was in a new job and assumed Jane had known what she was doing, but surely any researcher worth her salt would have checked Archives first? Even a country-based researcher could access the Archives database and request the archivists to download the images, so it wasn't as though she'd never used them before. Admittedly, some of the older film stock hadn't been digitised yet, but it had still been catalogued.

Archives would have been my first port of call for this story. Why wasn't it hers? Did she *want* an excuse to drive out to Galston?

Whatever the reason, ten minutes after I walked back into Ultimo (after stopping for delicious BBQ pork buns in Chinatown, just down the road), I had the shot list ready from the archived images.

I took it to Barry.

'McGowan, what've you got?'

'Recces were a wash out, but I have a shot list of archival stuff that will do just as well. Better, maybe.'

He took the print out with a surprised look on his face, as if he hadn't expected me to be competent. Ahah. He hadn't wanted me as the researcher. Tyler had put me in without asking him, I'd bet. Children's TV doesn't have much of a reputation in NewsCaff. They think we're airy fairy and flaky.

But Barry didn't comment out loud.

'Jack's producing this story,' he said. 'Jack! Come and meet Poppy.'

Before I met Tol, I used to fantasise about being assigned a producer who was gorgeous and single and not gay. Jack Wang was truly gorgeous, with those Eurasian cheekbones and deep dark eyes. He grinned at me and his eyes did that *flick* up and down me that straight men do to women, which meant that, astonishingly, he wasn't gay. The *flick* even lingered for a microsecond on my breasts *and* my face, which was nothing short of a miracle.

I smiled at him, feeling just a tiny bit flustered but not showing it. He was too sure of himself already, this one. I wasn't going to feed that ego. Besides, I had Tol.

'Hi, Poppy!' he said sunnily. 'You're taking over from Jane?' His face clouded appropriately at her name, but I got the feeling there'd been no real grief behind it.

'Yes-' I started, but Barry cut in.

'McGowan's been seconded from CHED.' That stands for Children's and Education, which is what long-term ABC people call ABC Kids.

'Just until you find a replacement,' I said firmly. They both looked at me with surprise.

'You don't want the job?' Barry asked.

'In my job I get to do documentary *and* drama *and* write the scripts,' I said, going for an explanation which would make sense to these driven news types. 'Can you offer me that here?'

'The only drama we've got is real,' Jack said. 'And *I* write the scripts. From your notes, of course.' He was grinning, but he meant it.

'Of course,' I said, mock humble.

The two other researchers, both women, had come over to join the conversation and take the chance to meet me. One was a strawberry blonde (at least this week—I suspected her hair was really mouse-coloured) in a short summer dress and the other was a buxom brunette who wore a hijab along with a very tight top and skinny jeans. They smiled at me and the one with the hijab said, 'We are but humble researchers, not fit to lick thy boots, oh mighty producer.'

'That's right,' Jack agreed. 'It's nice that everyone understands that.'

We all chuckled. Barry introduced me to the others: Claudia was the blonde and Meri the jeans girl.

I figured I might as well use the general good humour to poke a bit.

'What I don't understand is why Jane went on a recce at all,' I said. 'This story was better done from Archives.'

Meri snorted and Claudia rolled her eyes, but the men looked puzzled.

'Not to speak ill of the dead or anything,' Claudia drawled in a very posh accent (private school, Eastern suburbs money and, now that I looked, very expensive shoes), 'but Janey wanted to be a *News* researcher, in the midst of excitement and flurry and tension and all that shit. We spend half our lives on the phone and the other half in Archives, but that wasn't good enough for Janey. She wanted the fast lane.'

'That's why she moved from Orange in the first place,' Meri added, a little more kindly.

'That and her mum carked it finally,' Jack said. 'She'd been caring for her for about five years.'

That put a damper on things. The women moved back to their desks, Meri saying, 'Let me know if you need anything, Poppy,' over her shoulder as she went.

'They seem nice,' I said to Jack.

'They are.' He looked at the print out and nodded. 'Yep, good, Karen will requisition this footage from Archives. Good job. What about the interviews?'

I'd done a bit of checking on line.

'There's a firm in Alexandria which makes these new super-duper playgrounds for councils. I'm sure I can get a council Parks officer to talk about accidents going down or something like that. Then there's the CCA angle.'

He looked baffled, which was odd, because this had all been in Jane's notes.

'Chromated Copper Arsenate. Used to treat pine to stop it decaying. It's poisonous and that's why a lot of '70's play-grounds, you know, the climbing castles and jungle gyms made out of wood? That's why they were taken down. Jane lined up a scientist from the CSIRO.' I paused, considering. The more I looked at this story, the weaker it seemed. 'Jack, I just don't see why this is a *Daily Report* story. It's the sort of thing they do on daytime talk shows.'

He made a face. 'Jane was keen on it and it's all I've got for that Friday night soft slot. Find me something else in the next hour and I owe you one. Barry's all "in Jane's honour" but he won't care if we come up with something better.'

'What do you need?' I asked. 'What's your demographic? What are you trying to hit?'

'Okay,' he said, collecting his thoughts, surprised again that the kiddie researcher might actually know her job, 'Friday night is older viewers, so the nostalgia angle's not bad. We like it to be a bit feel-good to end the week on, but not super sentimental.'

'They're expecting a pair of tiger twins at the zoo,' I said.

'Perfect—but that's going to be covered by News when they're born.'

'But this week they're ultrasounding the tiger to see the twins inside,' I said.

Jack regarded me with humour brimming in his eyes. He really was very attractive.

'All right, I'll bite. How do you know?'

'I'm a *kiddie* researcher, mate,' I said. 'I keep in good with the zoo. CHED has a deal. They let me know in advance of anything interesting and we film it and can use it in any program we like—they get a copy of the footage for their archives. I got the heads up on Thursday last week that they'll be ultrasounding the tiger on Friday. It'll even be fresh news.'

Now it might seem to you that I was selling out CHED to ingratiate myself with my new bosses. But you would be wrong. Because our production timelines were so different, CHED wasn't going to use that tiger footage for another six months, in a show about veterinary science for a series on careers in science aimed at Year 10 kids. And this way, the cost of filming it would go to NewsCaff's budget instead of ours. And if I could wangle the right camera crew, I could be sure we'd get the kind of footage we needed.

'Dave and Terry could do it,' I added, nonchalantly. 'They've shot at the zoo for us before.'

Dave and Terry were an ex-News camera team who'd grown a little too old and staid to go running after fires and had been pastured off to children's shows. But they were technically terrific and could probably have shot and cut and scripted the whole story themselves blindfolded, they'd been in the business so long.

'Who've we got for talent?'

'Talent' is TV-speak for interviewees and other performers.

'The vet is good value; she's tiny, and she handles these huge animals like they're toys. And the tiger's keeper is full-on enthusiastic. He'll try to turn it into an ad for the zoo, but you can cut around that. We have archival footage of the albino cheetah cubs from last year, the lion cubs from the year before that, and tiger cubs from Melbourne Zoo.' I knew all this stuff off by heart. It had been the last story I worked on. I'd been planning to milk it for a *Launchpad* episode on baby animals.

'Okay,' Jack said. 'I'll clear it with Barry. Can the playground story and put the zoo up on the board. Then find me a closing story for Wednesday night's show. Nothing too sweet.'

And I was off and running in NewsCaff.

———

THE AFTERNOON WAS HECTIC.

Carol, the anchor, worked furiously at her desk and in the editing suite until twenty minutes before broadcast, when she went to get her makeup done. The reporters had been out in the field during the day and arrived back only to disappear into editing as well, along with their producers.

The whiteboard with the night's running order was changed four times by 4pm because of breaking news. The soft story at the end got bumped and replaced by a piece from Syria about the civil war. Jack caught that one and had to edit it on the fly. He kept calling out to know how to spell all the Syrian names and get him background on past events, and there I was, having read every piece of news about Syria for the last two months, because Syria is next to Jordan, and very near the place Tol was planning to dig, so I had been worried. I knew *everything*. Talk about serendipity. By the end of the day he was convinced I was the answer to his prayers.

It was expected that everyone stay for broadcast each night.

All the reporters were there as well as the producers and researchers and Tyler. Barry was in the control booth, of course, along with the director. And it was Carol's birthday, so there was wine and cheese.

I hadn't had much to do with the reporters. I knew them by sight, of course, from watching the show. I'd formed my own opinions of them well before I met them: Brad Charles was clever, quick-thinking and thought he was even more gorgeous that his six-foot blondness would warrant. He liked going for the jugular in interviews. Simon Forsyth was the opposite. He was the boy next door grown up, who soothed his subjects into revealing the secrets of their heart. He was great at human interest interviews and representing the man-in-the-street-confronting-the-corporate-menace.

Kate Agnetti was what a movie reviewer would describe as 'feisty'. She was smaller than most reporters, only average height, and her face had a delicate bone structure below beautifully cut natural red hair. Great in close up. She lulled interviewees, especially men, into underestimating her, and then stuck a knife in their guts. I quite liked her, although a couple of days in the office had shown that she was prepared to stick the knife into her co-workers if they didn't come up to her standards. I wondered how she and Jane had got on.

As we waited for the station promo to end and the show to start, I handed her a glass of chardonnay and asked her about Jane.

'Jane?' Kate shuddered and then bit her lip guiltily, looking over her shoulder to make sure no one had seen her. 'Sorry. Forgot she was dead for a minute.' She took a healthy swig of wine and shrugged. 'She drove me insane. Wanted to be two chums together because I come from Dubbo. Two country girls in the big city.'

Dubbo is a country town much like Orange. Kate grinned.

'Difference was, I got out of there when I was seventeen and never looked back.' She finished her wine. 'Poor Jane. She never quite got the hang of things around here. But if you want to know about her, ask Simon. She had quite a pash on him.'

'Really?' Maybe my voice revealed how unlikely a pairing I thought that was, because Kate chuckled.

'I didn't say he reciprocated. But she certainly tried!'

I couldn't resist. I just couldn't. As the baby of the team, I was the waitress, so I took the bottle over to Simon and offered to top up his glass. He put his hand over the top of it.

'Driving,' he explained, grinning a bit soppily and leaning in closer to me on the pretext of hearing better. From the smell of his breath, that wasn't the first drink he'd had this afternoon.

'Don't want to end up like Jane,' I said. I have no taste for the boy-next-door type. In fact, they tend to irritate me. I could cheerfully kick Hugh Grant in Notting Hill. Simon's practised flirtation just annoyed me.

He flinched. A real flinch.

'You know they don't think it was an accident?' I asked.

I swear he went pale.

'No,' he said. 'No. She wouldn't.'

Interesting.

'You think she killed herself?'

'No, no, she wouldn't-' He'd turned actually green. He slammed the glass down on the nearest desk and made for the door. I followed. He looked genuinely unwell.

He went into one of the office's unisex bathrooms. I waited, trying not to hear the sounds of vomiting. It all seemed a bit extreme, unless he had genuinely been fond of her... Behind me the title music started to play. I half turned to watch the monitor.

After the first story (the Syrian one), I knocked on the door and opened it cautiously.

'Are you all right?'

He was holding himself upright on the basin, his shoulders slumped.

'Are you sure she killed herself?' he asked, his voice flat.

'Why?'

He turned, face white, eyes huge. 'It was because of me, wasn't it?'

Ah.

'Why would you think that?'

Simon looked at me and I swear I could see the moment he decided to tell me all about it.

'We had a one-night stand,' he said.

'Let me guess. She didn't realise it was a one-night stand.'

He shook his head like a bull confused by the matador.

'She thought... I only slept with her because everyone could see she wasn't going to make it here. It was just a matter of time before Barry got rid of her. So it wasn't like fouling your own nest, you know?'

What a lovely image. But I knew what he meant. Office romances screwed up work.

'She was all for it—I didn't have to *seduce* her or anything. I didn't realise...'

'She took it seriously?'

'She was a *virgin*!' Mixed in with the incredulity were affront and a weird pride, as though she'd both insulted and complimented him.

'She was in love with you...'

'She thought it was "the real thing".' He turned back to the mirror and stared at himself, the natural vanity of the TV reporter resurfacing. He pulled a comb out of his pocket and neatened his hair. A good excuse for not looking me in the eyes. 'I tried to let her down gently, but she didn't want to accept it. She was getting a bit stalkerish. I suppose I was her grand passion...'

I could see, as calmness returned, so did ego. There was just a bit of him that liked the idea that Jane had killed herself because of him. It made me want to make him squirm.

'The police think that maybe she was murdered. And usually, when a woman is murdered, it's by her boyfriend or partner.'

He whirled around in shock and I smiled my best smile at him before stepping out of the bathroom and leaving him to stew in his own juices. I wished I could believe that he had killed Jane, but he was more likely to have revelled in any drama she created. Still. The gossip magazines had recently linked his name to a reality TV host, Morag Jones, and who knew how she had reacted to Jane's 'stalkerish' behaviour?

When Detective Chloe got around to calling me, I'd ask her.

———

WATCHING the show meant I didn't finish until 8pm. I understood, now, why Barry had been alone when I'd come in at 9 am. Meri told me they didn't start work until 10 or later usually, although if you had a story you were chasing you might work at any hour, particularly if the story was overseas with a big time difference.

Jack was staying back that night to organise a satellite interview with a guy in London who had chained himself to the top of the London Eye in protest against CCTV cameras invading British privacy.

I went home exhausted and found my lovely Tol had not only cooked dinner, he'd done my washing as well. This man was definitely a keeper.

———

I WAS at work at nine.

Barry was the only one there. Did that man never go home? He looked up and frowned as I came in.

'Oh, sorry, Poppy, should have told you, nine o'clock was just for yesterday. Ten is fine.'

'Ah,' I said, not commenting and therefore not lying.

I wanted to have a chance to go through the rest of Jane's notes before work started for real. Detective Chloe was going to call me today, I knew it.

I settled down at Jane's—at *my* desk, and methodically went through her in-tray and her drawers and all the files on her desk.

'What are you looking for?' Barry asked me, half suspicious.

'Just making sure there's nothing I'm supposed to follow up on. Interviews she might have set up, satellite time, that kind of thing.'

He perched his hip on the side of my desk and tapped a pencil against his thigh.

'You won't find anything.'

I raised my eyebrows at him.

'Frankly, you've done more useful work in one day than she did in four weeks. We were going to get rid of her.'

I winced at the turn of phrase and so did he, once he realised what he'd said.

'I just meant-'

'She wasn't any good?'

'Terrible. Still starry eyed and expecting big things to fall in her lap. What would you say a researcher's job is?'

I ticked it off on my fingers.

'Find the story, set the story up, make sure the story won't blow up in the reporter's or producer's face.'

He laughed, relaxing fully for the first time since I'd met him. 'Exactly. But she thought she was a crusading angel, fighting corruption.'

'Oh, dear.'

Now I want to be clear about this. I am a big believer in quality journalism and the ABC has the reputation (and the history) of being absolutely fearless in the pursuit of corruption or malice or evil. It has toppled governments, broken rings of conspiring police and politicians, and forced businesses to take responsibility for their mistakes. *But...* if you are a professional in this field, you don't *talk* about that kind of thing. You just do your job, and if you do your job well, these things will happen. That's how it works.

Someone who went around talking about fighting corruption in a newsroom full of cynical reporters...

'She sounds very *young*,' I said. Barry nodded.

'Money does that to you,' he said. 'Even the poor side of the family was rolling in it. Private school, private income, played at working because she liked the idea of the glamour of television. You'd think being a carer for her mum would have brought her down to earth, but I guess it's not quite as gritty when you have 24 hour nursing staff. She'd never faced life on her own before she came here.'

And then she died. Poor Jane.

'Men?' I asked. Did Barry know about Simon?

He shrugged. 'She was good looking enough, in a horsey kind of way. Camilla Parker-Bowles sort of thing. But if you'd told me she was a virgin I wouldn't have been surprised.'

Poor, poor Jane. Her great romance and no one had even noticed.

Chapter 5

Tuesday

At the bottom of Jane's bottom drawer, I found her personal items. The usual stuff, mostly: some make up, tampons, a few photographs of her and friends out in the country, a copy of her application to work at NewsCaff, and her address book.

I studied the photos with a sympathetic eye. As Barry had said, she was *jolie laide*, but with that healthy outdoorsy glow. And yet, not at all sensual, as some such women are. Good skin, good mid-brown hair, good teeth, not an ounce of oomph. Plain Jane. No wonder she'd yearned for glamour in her work life. The only notable feature of her face was highly arched eyebrows, the kind that were fashionable in the 1930s.

The friends were similarly middling; all wearing what even I could recognise as expensive country wear, but none shouting 'look at me'. They were just a bunch of nice, well-scrubbed country girls, even though none of them were younger than thirty. But all of the others had wedding rings.

Under the photos was one more manilla folder. I bent to pick it out of the drawer, expecting it to be as light as it was thin. But a hard heavy shape slipped out as I picked it up and I barely caught it before it hit the floor.

A laptop. An *expensive* laptop, high end and super fast.

That was weird.

Firstly, why didn't she have it with her? I don't go anywhere for work without my laptop. It'd be like cutting off my right arm to leave it behind.

Secondly, the ABC doesn't run to high-end, so this must be Jane's personal machine.

And thirdly... if it were Jane's personal laptop, why didn't Barry give it to the police? Maybe he just hadn't found it. Maybe nobody had searched her desk, since they hadn't let the police in.

Maybe Barry hadn't known it existed.

If it weren't ABC property, *I* could give it to the police. Or at least lend it.

But I'd better be sure it was Jane's before I handed it over, right?

It was so tempting to open it up right then and there but Tuesday turned out to be planning day and we were all called into the conference room to plot out the next week's stories.

One third federal politics, one third state news, one third everything else, including the soft stuff. Barry assigned Jack and the other Sydney producer, Marta, their targets first, then worked on Zoom with the producers from the other cities. Tyler sat at the corner of the table opposite Barry and threw a few words in here and there. I have to admit, he knew his stuff.

We researchers were part of the deal—it was our job to suggest stories in the first place, or to give background to producers, or to pull up facts and figures right then and there from the internet. It was fun. With the ideas flying and the deadlines looming, I could see why people got hooked on current affairs. Adrenaline addiction.

Nobody expected much from me at this first meeting, although I did suggest a follow up story about Syria based on a women's rights group there which boasted an ex-pat Mann Booker prize winner as their London spokeswoman.

At lunchtime, I slid the laptop and Jane's address book into my own computer bag and headed for Chinatown, but Meri and Claudia intercepted me.

'Come for lunch?' Meri asked.

It would have been stupid to say no.

We went to Paddy's Markettown, a couple of blocks away. Paddy's is a huge market, originally a farmers' market way back when, but now two-thirds cheap knock-offs and tat. It caters to tourists and teenagers and, in its surviving vegetable section, to migrants, especially Asian migrants, who can buy just about any of their homeland delicacies there. It's open from Thursday to Sunday. On top of this market is a mall. On the top floor of the mall is an Asian-style food hall, which has little sections of seating near each outlet. The whole place smells of star anise and chicken broth.

I must confess to a serious addiction to wonton noodle soup. I have very specific requirements. I like Shanghai style with a prawn and pork dumpling. No spices, but chives and ginger are okay. It should have lots of fresh vegetables (bok choy, Chinese broccoli, bean sprouts, carrots) and be sprinkled with dried onion. And, most importantly, the broth should be made on site from an actual chicken, not out of a stock powder.

Only one of the stalls in the food hall fitted these criteria, and it was one of my favourite places: the Golden Shanghai Noodle.

So I happily dipped into my wonton soup while Meri had salt and pepper squid and Claudia demolished a huge order of bbq pork and rice. Sydney has the best food in the world.

'So,' Claudia said with an evil grin, 'what's Nathan Castle really like?'

I groaned. A few months ago, a celebrity magazine had got hold of a photo of me with Nathan Castle, the pop star (aka Jonathan, my Aunty Mary's best friend's son), and decided it was a romance. The fact that it all happened in the middle of a murder investigation just made it juicier.

'Nice guy, family friend, no romance,' I said.

'Did you really identify the murderer?' Meri asked, agog.

I'd been hoping that they wouldn't know all the details, but they were news researchers, after all.

'I just helped the police with some information,' I mumbled, red faced. It had been a horrible time in my life and I hated to remember it. I had been far more involved than I would have liked to be.

'Damn!' Claudia laughed. 'We were hoping for some real goss.'

'It's all sub judice anyway,' I said.

One of the *good* things about working in television is that you lose any celebrity worship quickly, so they let it drop.

'Tell me about Jane,' I said.

Meri sighed.

'I feel like I ought to be sadder, you know? But she was driving us crazy.'

'You mean she was driving Jack crazy,' Claudia corrected her. 'He's a perfectionist,' she explained to me, 'and Jane...'

'She was enthusiastic,' Meri said, half in defence of Jane and half laughing.

'She was always *late*,' Claudia said, as if this was equivalent to being a murderer. Maybe, in a business which had an absolute deadline every day, it was.

'In a funny way,' Meri added, 'I wasn't surprised when she died.'

'Too good to live?' I asked, and then felt ashamed when Claudia laughed.

'No.' Meri slapped Claudia's arm with the back of her hand in remonstrance, and they smiled at each other. Very warmly. Sat the wind in that quarter? I wondered. Office romances are pretty common in TV—you spend so much time with your team that if there's mutual attraction it's almost inevitable.

'No,' Meri repeated. 'But a car accident? No surprise there. She just didn't seem that competent at life.'

'She couldn't read people,' Claudia added. 'She didn't understand why she put people's backs up or why no one rushed to be her friend. She wanted to be besties with us straight away, without even getting to know us. And she was *very* conservative.'

I decided to chance my arm.

'So she didn't approve of you two?' I wiggled my eyebrows at them.

Meri was startled. She looked at Claudia involuntarily, hand to her mouth. Claudia wasn't fazed. She tossed her long blonde hair back as if she were doing a Miss Piggy impersonation.

'God, are we that obvious?'

'Not *obvious*,' I said. And then I got the story of their lives and their romance and how they couldn't tell Meri's family about it and so on and so forth. I learnt a lot, some of which was very interesting. I didn't know that the story of Sodom was part of the Qur'an, for example.

Eventually, I brought the subject back to Jane.

'So Jane didn't approve either?'

Meri bit her lip and fidgeted with where the edge of her hijab met her cheek.

'No, she didn't approve. She pretended to, but you could see she was uncomfortable with it. She never figured it out—not like you. But she wanted to hang around with us after work and we had to tell her. We don't get to spend that much time together; we didn't want to waste it. I feel a bit guilty now. She just wanted to be friends.'

Claudia took Meri's hand, brought it down from her face and held onto it comfortingly.

'It's not our fault she's dead. Besides, it's just as well. She wasn't going to let it go.'

'Let what go?'

'She thought Meri should tell her parents. Bring it all out in the open.' She put a saintly tone on. 'Live honestly and truly! Let honour be your guide! That kind of crap.'

'Maybe she was right,' Meri said mournfully, her big brown eyes beginning to tear up. She had hardly touched her squid. 'Maybe I should be honest.'

'Don't do it,' I said. They looked at me with identical expressions of surprise.

'My parents are pathologically Catholic,' I explained. 'They still think I'm a virgin. Unless they ask me outright, I'm not going to tell them differently. I won't lie if they ask me, but I'm not going out of my way to cause them unnecessary pain. If they knew I was sleeping with my boyfriend, they would really believe I was going to Hell, and it would seriously grieve them. That's a terrible thing to do to someone.'

Meri sat up a bit straighter and nodded. 'That's what Jane didn't understand. That *they* would be hurt.'

'She didn't believe in secrets,' Claudia said. 'That's why she wanted to work in NewsCaff. To blow the lid off secrets.'

As we walked back to the office, I wondered if Jane had planned to blow the lid off a secret someone *really* wanted kept covered up.

Chapter 6

Tuesday

I didn't get a chance to look at Jane's laptop until after work. Then I did something which was probably, technically, illegal.

On the way home I stopped off at the big Officeworks store opposite Sydney Uni, taking a moment to enjoy the roosting white cockatoos which had transformed a fairly ugly gum tree just inside the Uni gates into a fairytale tree with living blossoms. Like most Sydneysiders, I hate cockatoos (so loud, so destructive) but I had to admit they made a pretty sight.

I bought a 2 terabyte hard drive and as soon as I got home I sat down at my dining table and fired up Jane's laptop.

It was password protected. Of course. I tried the obvious ones: password, Jane, Mancus, NewsCaff, dailyreport, her birthdate from the employment application I'd found in her drawer, Orange, a few others.

Nothing. The problem was I didn't know Jane well enough.

I'd have to hand it over to Detective Chloe. No doubt her tech experts could open it up.

Before I shut it down, on a whim, I typed in 'smileyface'.

Bingo.

It was really pathetic that a 40 year old woman had 'smileyface' as her password. But I was in.

Now came the illegal part. Up until that moment, I could have argued that I thought this was a work computer. But on the Finder window the hard drive was called 'Jane's laptop', whereas I knew that ABC laptops just identified the department and a number (such as NewsCaff7). I took a deep breath and plugged the hard drive in, and copied the entire contents of her hard drive across.

I was pretty sure I'd hear from Detective Chloe soon, and I wanted—well, what did I want?

Part of me, I realised, was feeling very protective towards Jane. I knew what it was like to yearn for honour and right and justice; the last six months of my life had been a horrible example of what happened when people forgot those things because of self-ishness and greed. Part of me *respected* Jane for holding onto those ideals so strongly. And another, more cynical, part of me felt like shaking her retrospectively and saying, 'Wake up to yourself, honey, you're laying yourself wide open.'

Wide open to death, as it turned out.

The copying was almost finished when my phone rang. Detective Chloe.

'Hello, Detective Inspector, how are you?' I said in my very best manners voice.

'Yes. What have you got for me?'

'I have Jane's laptop.'

There was a moment's silence and I felt quite smug.

'Have you looked at it?'

'No,' I said. 'But I've cracked the password.'

'Where are you?'

'At home. *My* house, in Wells St.'

'Fifteen minutes,' she said, and hung up.

Detective Chloe knew my house inside and out. A woman had been killed here, while I was still renovating. Tol's last girlfriend, Julieanne. I looked across at the stairway. At the time, there had been no balustrade, and no wooden boards, and Julieanne had lain all night sprawled half in and half out of a hole in the floor.

Friends had urged me to sell the house. But I *loved* that house, and I felt that if I sold it the murderer would have managed to destroy something else. Besides the more practical reason that it's hard to sell a house where someone has been murdered.

No, that wasn't important. The point was that Julieanne's ghost had no reason to haunt me. I'd found her murderer and brought him to justice. Even though Julieanne and I hadn't liked each other, I didn't feel that her ghost would hold any animosity towards me. But I was glad the new floorboards covered up the actual spot where she'd been killed.

'Eternal rest grant unto her, O Lord, and let perpetual light shine upon her,' I said.

The computer beeped. Hastily, I unplugged the hard drive and hid it in my laptop bag, then went to the kitchen and got coffee and cake.

I carried the tray out of the kitchen just as Tol ushered Detective Chloe through the front door.

'Got a key, I see,' she said to him. He grinned.

I flushed a little. I hadn't thought twice about giving Tol a key. When the locksmith put the new locks in I'd ordered four extra keys: one each for Tol, Annie, my parents and my friend Alex.

'You're reacting fast if this is just a suicide,' I said.

'We got the toxicology back,' she said, walking through my tiny lounge room and making straight for the table where I'd set up the laptop.

'And?' I poured out coffee for the three of us while Detective Chloe examined the computer. Tol kissed me and took a mug. He inhaled the steam thankfully. Tol is a coffee man; the quality of the coffee I kept had gone up significantly since I met him.

'Vodka and speed,' Chloe said, settling down at the table. 'A lethal mix—more than enough to kill her. She was dead before she went over the bridge. But it might still be suicide.'

My hand trembled as I poured and a little coffee went on the table top. Tol grabbed a paper napkin to mop it up, and hugged my shoulders as he went by to put the napkin in the garbage. I *was* upset. I really didn't want Jane to have been murdered.

'Not suicide,' I said. 'Not that way. Jane was too much a straight arrow to put other people at risk by driving in that condition.'

'But once she'd taken the mixture, she might not have been able to make good decisions,' Chloe countered.

'Do you *want* this to be suicide?'

Tol came back and leaned on the wall next to me, silent but supportive. He and Detective Chloe had had their problems in the past, and he always acted very protective towards me when she was around.

'I'd *always* prefer a suicide over a murder,' she flashed. 'Wouldn't you?'

She was right. Of course. But...

'Not suicide. Not Jane.'

'Well,' Chloe said, 'let's have a look at this, anyway.'

The computer had gone to sleep and you needed the password to wake it up. I didn't make her ask me.

'Smileyface, all one word lower case,' I said.

She typed it in and waited for the screen to clear.

'I can't believe you didn't examine this.'

I held up my hand and put the other over my heart.

'Scout's honour.'

Chloe sat down and absently took one of the coconut slices (thank you, Aunty Maree) from the tray as she looked through the list of documents. She produced a thumb drive and started copying anything which looked interesting.

'Is that legal?' I asked innocently. She fixed me with those clear blue eyes. Sometimes I think she likes me and sometimes I think she finds me very irritating.

'Are you currently in possession of this computer?'

'I guess.'

'Do you freely give your consent to me copying material from it?'

'Sure.'

'Then it's admissible in court, even if it's not legal in terms of copyright law, and that's all I care about.'

She turned back to the screen and checked Jane's browsing history for the past week.

Sites about horses. The Mancus' company site. Sites about playgrounds. Sites about sheep dogs. Sites about Syria.

'That was for work,' I offered helpfully. Chloe narrowed her eyes at me, but let me look over her shoulder.

An internet porn site.

Now that was very strange. Very strange indeed. Particularly as it was gay male porn.

'Must have been for work,' I said uncertainly. I mean, I know people do watch porn online, but *Jane*? It just didn't fit. She was the kind of woman who could probably have an orgasm over George Clooney in a coffee ad.

'Mm,' Chloe said.

The last two days there were only business sites: the Tax Office, the Australian Securities and Investments Commission (which is the stock exchange and companies' watchdog), the Australian Securities Exchange, the ABN register (Australian Business Number registry).

'Maybe she was thinking of starting her own business,' Tol said. 'I had to get an ABN when I started consulting work. I looked at all those sites then.'

Detective Chloe shrugged. 'I'll check out if she applied.' Reluctantly, she closed the computer down and turned to me. 'Did you find anything else in her papers?'

'Not exactly. But I did notice something odd.'

'Mm?'

'I had to go out to do the recce that Jane was on when she died.'

That got her attention. She turned and stared at me.

'They still did the story?' Non-TV people are always astonished at the pragmatism of the industry.

I shrugged. 'So I went and had a look at the bridge while I was there. She was going the wrong way.'

'What do you mean?'

I explained about how Jane shouldn't have been anywhere near Galston Gorge, but particularly shouldn't have been coming from the direction of Hornsby Heights.

'So where did she go first?'

'It would have been work-related. Jane was a straight arrow. She wouldn't have taken work time for personal reasons.'

Detecive Chloe sat back in her chair and regarded me.

'Tell me about her.'

So I told her everything I'd managed to pick up.

Detective Chloe nodded. 'Well, with any luck we'll have everything we need right here.' She patted the computer.

'You shouldn't keep it in the house,' she said, frowning, 'but it would be good if we could find it again if we needed to subpoena it. Don't give it back to the Mancuses.'

'Ok.' I wondered what to do if someone asked me outright if I'd seen Jane's computer. Would I—*should* I—lie for Detective Chloe?

Then she spent fifteen minutes cross-examining me about the office staff and Jane's relationships with them. I left out the relationship between Claudia and Meri. There was no way those two would kill to cover it up—they hadn't even been upset with me when I guessed. But otherwise I was forthcoming and detailed, especially about the affair with Simon and its aftermath.

Detective Chloe left in a good humour and quite approving of me for not tampering with the evidence. It made me a little guilty. I turned back to find Tol regarding me with a knowing eye.

'What did you do?'

'What do you mean?' I went into the kitchen and served us two bowls of the casserole I'd put in the slow cooker that morning. Working late meant no proper cooking when I got home.

'There is no way on earth that you would have broken that password and not looked at the files.'

'Well I didn't, so there, smarty pants!' I put my nose in the air and took the food through to the dining table while Tol put out place mats and cutlery. I ducked back to the kitchen for the salad waiting in the fridge.

'So what *did* you do?'

There was such humour and affection in his voice (and so much knowledge of me) it was a bit scary, frankly.

I said, 'I copied the entire hard disk onto a back up hard drive.'

He laughed until he had tears in his eyes, and then he kissed me.

'That's my girl.'

———

FOR VARIOUS REASONS into which I will not delve too deeply, I had no opportunity to look at Jane's files until the next morning, after Tol had left for work.

We weren't exactly living together. We were just spending most nights in the same bed. Usually mine, sometimes his. He only lived five minutes' drive away, so it was easy for him to nip back home in the mornings to shower and dress.

But it made me wonder how long this phase was going to last. I'd lived alone for thirteen years, and I'd thought that sharing my space (particularly my little house) with someone else would be very, very hard. Yet it was proving to be so, so easy. Almost too easy. I kept waiting for something to go bad.

I put that thought out of my head and plugged the hard drive into my computer—my desktop, in my little office upstairs.

The list of documents wasn't that interesting, but of course I headed straight for the emails. None of them were work related, which confirmed for me that Jane had had another laptop—or else did all her work emailing from the office, strange as that may have seemed. Most of the emails were to friends back in

Orange, and they were the ones I wanted to read. Jane's friends were close, obviously. If she were depressed enough to kill herself, she would have given them some clue.

Chapter 7

Wednesday/Thursday/Friday

I'd figured that whatever had happened to Jane had occurred after she came to Sydney, so I started with the messages she'd sent from four weeks ago.

The first two weeks were all about the new job, the new apartment, what it was like for a country girl in the city ('I've got hay fever!' she exclaimed to her best buddy, Melissa. 'I've handled hay all my life without a sniffle and now I've got hay fever! I'm sure it's the pollution.' She was probably right.)

Then there were a series of complaints about how Claudia and Meri and someone called Tamara (presumably the one off with flu) were just not very friendly and never invited her out after work. That went on for about a week and stopped abruptly, I suppose because Claudia and Meri confessed the truth. I was glad to see that Jane hadn't relayed their secret even to her best friend. She'd just said, 'They have their reasons, I daresay,' when Melissa asked, and left it at that.

And then there was a heartbreaking series of messages about Simon. The initial excitement, the crush, the first contact, the first night together, and then the crash and burn.

I'd been right—she told her friend Melissa everything.

I felt bad reading it; it was none of my business, it was private, it was like eavesdropping on a sixteen year old. But although she was heart-broken, devastated, humiliated... she didn't sound depressed in the clinical sense.

'I guess I have to just pick myself up and get back on track,' one email said. That didn't sound suicidal to me, but I knew that people who were considering suicide often acted more cheerful once they'd made the decision.

Later in the same message, there was another suggestive section about a quite different matter.

Unfortunately, it was clear she was following up some earlier conversation, either by phone or text.

The message was full of 'Now you know what the situation is' and 'As I explained' and 'what do you think I should do?', but maddeningly silent on the actual problem.

I changed directories and read Melissa's reply. She was a sensible woman, and she advised Jane to 'talk it over with them but *don't* get too emotional. They're not going to like the fact that you've found out, so tread carefully and don't threaten them. And why not come home for the weekend and get away from Simon and everything to do with the Daily Report?'

Melissa knew her Jane. But, oh, the curiosity! Talk it over with whom?

Detective Chloe would be all over this like a rash. She would track down Melissa (not that hard, her email address was mhunter2866@hotmail.com.au). I had a hunch, and I was right. 2866 turned out to be the postcode for a small town called Amaroo, near Orange. If Detective Chloe couldn't find Melissa Hunter in Amaroo, I'd be very, very surprised.

But that didn't stop me from contacting her myself. In my position as inheritor of Jane's desk.

I emailed her with a simple expression of sympathy and told her I'd found photos of her with Jane and her friends in Jane's desk and what did she think I should do with the photos? Perfectly reasonable. I included my phone numbers and home address, just in case she wanted to contact me directly.

It's not that I wanted to solve Jane's death myself. I had every confidence Detective Chloe could do that, particularly now she had Melissa's contact details and all the information about Simon and Jane. It was more that, since I'd plunked my bottom down in Jane's chair, she'd become increasingly real to me. I wanted to know more about her. I wanted to be reassured that she hadn't been destroyed by coming to the city. That her life had been worth living, even if it had been cut short.

Well, that was what I told myself. My mother would have said it was my curiosity leading me astray.

Detective Chloe had *asked* me to help. It was a whisper-thin excuse, but what the hell.

I figured Melissa was my best source of information.

Then I realised she wasn't my only source of information. Although the documents on the laptop were pretty boring—tax records, her application for the Daily Report job, her exercise diary, that sort of thing—I still had her address book. I'd forgotten to give it to Detective Chloe.

I found Melissa's name easily enough, and the other friends she'd emailed with. These older addresses were written in purple ink. I was surprised it didn't have sparkles in it, like the ink in my favourite pen when I was fourteen.

There were newer, Sydney addresses, too, written in blue. Doctor, dentist, ob/gyn—my God, she was organised! There were family names, too—all the Mancus clan, from the patriarch, William, to the flippety party girl, Paige, who hadn't reached 18 yet but was already all over the tabloids.

It surprised me that the family names were written in blue, but then I realised—before she left Orange, she would have used her mother's address book if she needed family contacts. She had transferred these to her own address book before she left Orange, using the new grown up blue pen.

I wondered what her very sophisticated city relatives had thought of her.

———

Thursday

I had taken the laptop to work but I left it in my car. Turned out that NewsCaff had some of the highly desirable and hotly contested parking spaces, and that researchers were eligible to use them if they were prepared to use their own car on recces. Since I routinely used my own car at *Launchpad*, I was very happy. No more V8 tanks. And within the strict security of the ABC, the laptop would be safe in my boot.

In the middle of the morning, when I was deep in trying to set up an interview with the leader of the State opposition to get comment on rumours there was going to be a leadership spill, a tall man walked into the office and simply stopped, as if waiting for us all to respond.

He looked vaguely familiar. Silvered hair, about sixty, *beautiful* suit, tanned skin, a strong nose and high eyebrows which gave him a supercilious air. The eyebrows—so like Jane's and yet so unlike hers in expresssion—triggered my memory. This was a Mancus. And not just any Mancus, but William, the head of the clan himself. He might look 60, but he was closer to 70 and, I remembered, he could waltz in here because he was a member of the ABC Board of Management, appointed by the current government.

I should have let Barry notice him and intervene, but I couldn't resist. I went over to him.

'Mr Mancus,' I said. 'I'm so sorry about Jane.'

He turned and looked down at me, in every sense. I smoothed my working-class hackles and smiled at him, putting my hand out.

'I'm Poppy McGowan.'

He shook hands perfunctorily.

'I'm here for Jane's things.' His voice was almost without tone. Not robotic, just flat.

Barry had realised who this was and hurried over to take charge.

'Mr Mancus. Barry Lowe. I'm so sorry about-'

'I'm here for Jane's things.'

'The police-' I began.

He ignored me and concentrated on Barry.

'Jane's possessions, if you please.' It wasn't a request.

'Poppy,' Barry said. 'Get Jane's things for Mr Mancus.'

He wasn't kowtowing, but he wasn't resisting this arsehole, either. But why should he? He didn't have a Detective Inspector breathing down his neck.

'Sure,' I said.

I collected Jane's photos and notes and manilla folders and handed them over in an untidy heap to Barry.

'Get a box,' he said.

I found an empty photocopy paper box. Barry dumped the stuff into it and handed it over to Mancus. At least he didn't offer to carry it down to the car for him.

'Her computer?' Mancus asked.

I kept quiet.

'Researchers usually take their laptops with them when they go on recces,' Barry explained, sotto voce because he was talking about Jane's last trip. 'So I assume it was in her car...' He straightened and gained a little authority. 'And of course her desktop is the property of the ABC.'

Mancus nodded, turned around and left.

'Arsehole,' I said.

'Arsehole who controls the budget for this unit,' Barry said. And that explained why no one was co-operating with the cops.

The penny dropped, belatedly.

'*That's* why Jane got the job!'

Barry looked harassed and bit embarrassed.

'On paper it looked like she had the skills!' he protested. 'She'd been working in Orange for years. Tyler wasn't in favour, I have to admit, but I thought it couldn't hurt...'

Poor, poor Jane. Thrust into a job she couldn't handle because of internal ABC politics. I felt quite cross with Barry.

———

THAT NIGHT TOL was giving a fund-raising lecture to a group of archaeology enthusiasts at the Museum, so I had the night to myself, and I spent it catching up on paperwork and correspondence. I received a lovely email from Melissa Hunter, thanking me for my offer and agreeing that she would like to have the photos back. Perfect. I wrote back and explained about Mr Mancus coming into the office and demanding everything.

'My producer thought it was okay, but is he really Jane's next of kin? Should her things have gone to someone else?' I asked. 'He didn't seem to be particularly grief-stricken.'

Within half an hour I had a reply.

'Mr Mancus is definitely *not* Jane's next of kin. That is her grandmother, Mr Mancus' mother.' She gave me Mrs Mancus' address and phone number and advised me to contact her if I found anything else of Jane's.

I got the impression that Melissa also thought that William Mancus was an arsehole.

'Thanks, Melissa,' I wrote back. 'I appreciate this. The whole office has been shocked by Jane's death and by the rumours that it wasn't an accident.'

Almost immediately I got an email back.

'Poppy, I can't believe that Jane killed herself. I knew she was down, but surely she wouldn't do something so drastic?'

Now that was interesting.

I wrote back. 'You would know better than I would, I'm sure. You were so obviously her best friend.'

Nothing. No reply, no bounce back. Just silence.

―――――

In the morning I checked my mail before leaving, as I always do. There was a message from Melissa, time- stamped at 3.16 am. She couldn't sleep after my questions.

'Dear Ms McGowan,' she said, quite formal considering the tone of her earlier messages, 'I will be coming to Sydney for Jane's funeral. I hope to be able to meet you there. I may have some idea about why Jane might have been very upset; I will be talking to someone about that before the funeral to confirm it, and then we will know the truth. Thank you for your kindness,

yours sincerely

Melissa Hunter.'

She sounded terrible. I didn't bother writing back. I dug out Jane's address book and called her.

Her husband answered the phone.

'Sorry, Melissa's gone to Sydney for a couple of days,' he said. 'For a friend's funeral.'

'Do you know where she's staying?'

'Oh, she'll be at the Wentworth. We always stay there. Do you want me to take a message in case I speak to her before you do?'

I gave him my name and number and a message asking Melissa to call me.

The receptionist at the Sofitel Wentworth, a grand hotel in the middle of Sydney much beloved of country people, told me she hadn't checked in yet. She probably wouldn't be there until after lunch time, given how small the planes were that flew to Orange.

I would keep ringing until I contacted her, I promised myself. I didn't know why I was feeling so panicky, but I didn't want Melissa confronting someone by herself.

But why shouldn't she? Then I realised, like Melissa, a big part of me just didn't believe Jane had killed herself. Which meant that she had been murdered, and Melissa might be confronting her killer.

Chapter 8

Friday

I struggled a bit with my conscience at this point.

As I got ready for work I argued it back and forth: Melissa had trusted me with information. Chloe trusted me to keep her informed.

In the end, I decided that the only important person was Jane; and the only important thing was catching her killer. So I rang Detective Chloe and filled her in.

Or rather, I tried. But her phone was answered by her offsider, Detective Sergeant Martin (Steven Martin is his full name, poor sod). While Detective Chloe and I had reached a working agreement in the last few months, Martin didn't like me. He'd made a fool of himself by arresting Tol for something he didn't do, and he hadn't liked being made to look a fool when the murderer turned out to be someone else altogether. And he held a grudge. So when I told him about Melissa, he just said, 'Another one of your theories, McGowan?' and hung up.

I swore a bit, then sent a text to Detective Chloe's mobile asking her to call me, but she didn't call or text back. Bloody Martin probably intercepted it.

Work that day was frantic, and I was only saved from being completely overwhelmed by the return from sick leave of Tamara, the other researcher. She was a quirky young thing, about twenty-two, with striped black and pink hair and a Japanese schoolgirl meets goth look. And I knew her; she had been a civilian researcher for the police. In fact, I'd told her about the research opening here. But then she'd been called Gladys.

'Hey, McGowan,' she said to me when we met. 'Thanks for the tip off about the job.'

'I thought your name was Gladys?'

'That was just to annoy Martin. It was his Nan's name, and he *hated* calling me that.'

That made me laugh. She was tough and competent. 'So are you really named Tamara?'

'Fuck no.' She winked at me. 'I am a woman of constant mystery.' Then she grinned. 'It's really Karen, but honestly! I can't deal with that. Could you?'

Fair point.

———

FRIDAY IS A BIG NEWS DAY—POLITICIANS often time contentious announcements for the weekend so that people will pay less attention to them; Friday and Saturday news ratings are always lower than Monday to Thursday. It shoots up again on

Sunday, but by then a Friday announcement is old news, unless it's very controversial.

Today we had the leader of the opposition announcing that there would be a leadership spill. What was nice was that I'd already organised an interview with her for that afternoon, so although everyone got the doorstop announcement at Parliament House, we got the in-depth stuff. Jack was very pleased with me. Barry was very pleased as well, because Tyler had to ask him nicely to release some of the footage for the prime time news broadcast, and this put him ahead in whatever game of one-upmanship they were playing.

And I wondered if me organising that interview had actually set the timeline for the announcement. She knew she was guaranteed a good long interview on a respected current affairs show— perfect opportunity to explain why she should be retained as leader and how the challenger, a dinosaur from the old days of party politics, was a bad choice for everyone. We'd played right into her hands, in one sense. In another, we'd anticipated breaking news and scooped the other stations.

It was a heady thought, that I might have influenced the larger world, and I understood why people became addicted to this job. But it also made me feel a bit sick that a phone call from a lowly researcher at the ABC could have any influence on something this important.

We were all scurrying around organising other comments: the Premier, the challenger, the head of the national party, the head of the state party (no, that's not the same as the leader of the parliamentary party)... so it was mid-afternoon before I got a chance to call the Wentworth again.

To my surprise, I got straight through to Melissa.

'Oh, Miss McGowan,' she said, sounding flustered. 'I'm sorry I didn't get back to you. Don't worry about that email I sent you. Everything's fine.'

'You said you might know why Jane died,' I prompted.

'No, no, I was quite wrong about that. I'm sure.' She was trying hard to *sound* sure, at any rate.

'If there's any reason you can't talk now, I could call back later.'

'Oh, no, that won't be necessary. I'm sure that everything will get sorted out. I hate to think it, but perhaps Jane did- well...'

I wasn't sure if what Chloe had told me was confidential, but Melissa needed to be on her guard. 'Jane had speed and vodka in her system. Enough to kill her. Do you really think she would have driven like that?'

She was silent, but I could hear her uneven breathing. That had shocked her.

'No,' she said faintly. 'No, but-' There was a noise in the background. Someone knocking at her door? 'Oh, sorry, I've got to go now. I'll be in touch.' She hung up.

I looked at the receiver, not sure how to interpret what had just happened. Had someone threatened her to make her keep quiet? Or persuaded her that everything was just peachy keen somehow? She hadn't sounded stupid—but she had sounded 'nice'. The sort of person who would think the best of someone she knew. That was a ridiculous assumption to make about someone I'd never met. On the other hand, she'd been Jane's best friend, and Jane had been as naïve as a baby.

———

THE INTERVIEW WAS a stunning success because Carol managed to get the opposition leader to relax enough to reveal what she *really* thought about her rival. It wasn't pretty, but by God it was news. So good that the other channels bought snippets of it for their late-night news programs and we just knew it would be all over the newspapers tomorrow. When one politician uses phrases like 'horrible little weevil with wandering hands' and 'morals of a rattlesnake' about someone in their own party, you know the fur is going to fly.

So we all had a glass of wine to celebrate after the broadcast. I noticed, as I handed the glasses around, that Miss-Not-Karen was a bit smitten with Simon the Boy Next Door. She actually giggled at something he said, and put her hand on his arm. He smiled down at her with far too much appreciation, considering he was around fifteen years older than she was.

And I wondered how she'd felt about Jane and Simon. Drugs aren't uncommon in TV, especially speed, which lets people work on when the hours get long. I know it was pure stereotyping, but 'Tamara' struck me as someone who might know how to get speed if she wanted it. After all, she had worked for the police, and had had access to a literal database of drug dealers.

I couldn't see it, though. Gladys/Tamara/Karen was too shrewd to believe Simon was genuinely interested in Jane. And then there was that TV woman he was seeing. Tamara (I had to settle on one name, and it might as well be the one everyone else was using) was just too *smart* to do something this stupid. After all, it wasn't guaranteed that Jane would die from that drink.

Which was interesting in itself.

Chapter 9

Saturday/Sunday

Oh joy, oh bliss, the weekend!

Tol and I pottered around on Saturday—went down to The Rocks market, which stretches from Sydney Harbour up to the oldest part of the city. It's full of tourist crap, but it also features fantastic gourmet food like lemon myrtle-infused caramelised raspberry vinegar. Yum. And single origin bush honey from ironbark trees (so dark, so delicious). And deeply sinful chocolate fudge with macadamia nuts. And marinated wild olives... you get the picture. Did I mention Sydney has the best food in the world?

On a fabulous early summer day with a light wind from the harbour leavening the sunshine, it's hard to imagine a better way to spend a couple of hours.

Sunday I worked in my little garden (*my* garden!) while Tol went home and did his washing. It gave me a chance to compare being alone in my house to being with him in my house. I liked both. But when Tol was there... oh, who was I kidding? I was besotted with the man.

I thought of Jane, in love with a—a bounder. An old-fashioned word, but accurate. I considered calling Detective Chloe again, but what the hell. She'd asked my help. If she wanted to talk to me, she'd call me. She had all the same information that I did about Melissa. She could follow it up fine without my help.

Tol came back for dinner (roast lamb and veggies followed by rhubarb crumble and ice cream, and the raspberry vinegar as a jus).

I was serving up the crumble when someone knocked on the door.

Detectives Chloe and Martin. What on earth?

I ushered them in but they didn't sit down. That was unsettling. When police officers refuse to sit down there is bad news.

'What is it?'

'Melissa Hunter,' Martin said. 'You rang her on Friday afternoon at 2.30.'

I nodded. Tol got up from the table and came to stand behind me. I didn't quite lean back on him for support, but it was nice to have him there.

'She left her hotel room immediately after that call and hasn't been seen since,' Detective Chloe said.

Melissa. It wasn't my fault. She was an adult and could make her own decisions. But I wondered if I was ever going to believe that if Melissa turned up dead, too.

Chloe let the silence lie. I knew that technique. Silence is a great way to get people to talk. But I had nothing to hide and no reason not to talk.

'Just before she hung up, I heard something and she said she had to go, as though there were someone at the door.'

'Why did you call her?' Martin, being his usual sunny self.

'You *know* why I called her, Detective Sergeant Martin,' I said. 'I told you all about it on Friday morning.'

Detective Chloe looked sideways at him. Not happy.

'I logged that call,' Martin said defensively. 'But she wasn't making any sense. She just said that Melissa Hunter was coming to Sydney.'

He hadn't even listened to me properly.

'And I texted *you*,' I said to Chloe.

'I was planning to call you tomorrow,' she said, on the back foot and not liking it. 'What did you want to say to me?'

'I wanted to tell you that Melissa Hunter thought she knew why Jane had died and was going to confront the person responsible.'

'Oh, fuck,' Martin said.

'Tell me about your conversations with her,' Chloe said, deadpan.

I recounted the exchange of emails and our brief chat.

'So she didn't really know anything,' Martin said, trying to make himself feel better about not listening to me.

'She *said* she didn't. But-'

70

Detective Chloe held up a hand to stop me.

'All right. Do you have any idea where she might be?'

How I wished I did. I shook my head and clasped my hands around the fading warmth of my dessert bowl.

'There's just one thing I really want to know,' Tol said.

'What?' Her tone was resigned. She knew she owed us.

'How did Jane ingest the speed and vodka?'

He was right. That was the crux of the matter. If she'd taken tablets, then it was suicide.

'Dissolved in an energy drink,' Martin said grudgingly.

We both digested that in silence. Not a pretty picture. I thought of Claudia and Meri, drinking V all day long, and imagined Jane doing the same, wanting to fit in. Maybe taking some from the office fridge with her as she went off to her recce. For a moment, I toyed with the idea that the spiked drink had been meant for someone else—but Melissa's disappearance made that unlikely. It was increasingly clear that Jane had been murdered. I could tell Detective Chloe thought so.

'One thing. How did you get Melissa Hunter's email address?' Detective Chloe demanded.

Ah. The question I didn't want her to ask. Time for the exact truth rather than the full truth.

'I found Jane's address book. Hold on, I'll get it for you.'

I headed up the stairs to my office where the book was still in my laptop bag.

'And copies of the emails,' she called up after me.

'Okay.'

———

I PRINTED off the emails and heard Tol offer coffee or rhubarb crumble. When I came back, before I handed them to her I said, 'There's something else.'

I told her how William Mancus came in and took all of Jane's stuff.

'Photos, everything,' I added.

'The laptop?'

I brought the laptop out from under the emails and saw a flicker of satisfaction on her face.

'It was in my car, and he didn't ask. Barry assumed it had been destroyed in the crash and I didn't contradict him.'

'Good.' They turned to leave.

I hesitated.

'Um...'

'What *now*?' Martin snapped.

'You're investigating Melissa Hunter's disappearance because of her friendship with Jane, right?'

'Yes. She was on our list of people to interview.'

'So that means that Jane's laptop is evidence in that investigation, and as a good citizen I should hand it over to you... You're not looking for Jane's sources, are you? Just for her emails with Melissa.'

'Quite right,' Detective Chloe said, a gleam of humour in her eyes. She took the laptop and tucked it under her arm.

I just wanted to get that thing out of the house. As though it were cursed.

Chapter 10

Monday

I t was time to set the cat among the pigeons. Tyler made a
good cat.

I went into his massively untidy office early on Monday morning. As always, he was on the phone. He waved a hand at me to
sit down, so I did, and listened unashamedly to the conversation, which was about a story he was setting up with a stringer
in London. The protester guy was still on the London Eye and
had become something of a local hero; Tyler wanted vox pops
(quick man-in-the-street interviews—you know, 'What do you
think of this protest?').

He plunked the phone down, clapped his hands together once
and actually smiled at me.

'Come to ask for Jane's job permanently?' he asked smugly.

'No. Come to tell you that Jane was murdered and tell you that
her best friend, who thought she knew why, disappeared on
Friday and hasn't been seen since.'

He stared at me, incredulous.

If there was one thing I was sure of, it was that Tyler hadn't killed Jane. He had the ethics of a boa constrictor when it came to news, but he just didn't *care* enough about anything else to kill someone. And I didn't see any reason why the substantial information-gathering resources of the ABC couldn't be put onto this case. What was the media for, after all?

'I thought she drove off the bridge because she was drunk and the Mancuses wanted it all covered up,' he said. 'Simon's mate at the coroner's office said her blood alcohol reading was off the chart. That's why we've been fighting the cops on the subpoena. Too many journos drink; sooner or later some of them are going to cark it. If we let them have Jane's notes it'll set a precedent and maybe someday some informant will get it in the neck as a result.'

'Energy drink plus vodka plus speed. Dissolved into the drink. In the middle of the working day. You think that sounds like Jane?'

'Shit no. She was Miss Goody Two-Shoes.'

He sat back in his chair, brooding, then sat forward and picked up a pen, poising it over his notepad.

'Who's this best friend?'

For a moment I saw a younger Tyler, the ace reporter who had clawed his way up the news ladder. Fair enough. I gave him everything, even telling him about the laptop. I put the hard drive down on the desk.

'But you can't let anyone from Daily Report know about this,' I said.

'Why not?'

I looked him straight in the eye. 'Because the energy drinks are kept in the office fridge.'

He froze, then nodded, the overhead light shining off his bald spot and making him seem, for a moment, oddly vulnerable.

'I'll put Gina onto it. You can back her up.' Yes! Gina was a great reporter. And now I could pull any ABC resource I needed.

'In my spare time,' I said sarcastically.

'You're doing all right. Making yourself useful. You can find time.'

Translation: you are a terrifically efficient and valuable member of staff, so we will overwork you. Typical ABC.

———

THAT NIGHT TOL and I went to a secret jazz and blues club in Marrickville. Yes, I said secret. Sort of. A few months before, the club had had its licence pulled by the council because of fire regulations, so they weren't supposed to be holding any concerts. On the other hand, there was no law against the proprietor, who lived above the premises, holding a party and inviting a *lot* of people, who were only too happy to chip in $25 each towards the entertainment. Everyone brought their own food and drinks and settled in happily, chatting as though it really was a party. The atmosphere was helped by the decoration, which took the word 'kitsch' to a whole new level.

You had to be on the secret mailing list—friends of friends of friends—to get an invite, and it was always great music, with the extra frisson of doing something slightly illegal thrown in.

Tonight the act was Pugsley Buzzard, a honky-tonk piano player who combined talent with very funny original songs, a gravel voice worthy of Tom Waits, and the good sense to know when to sing someone else's song for a change of pace.

'So I was thinking...' Tol said in the break between sets.

'Mmm?' I sipped champagne and orange juice and gazed at him sappily.

'I was thinking it would make more sense if I just moved in for the duration. Since I'm giving up my flat anyway when I go to Jordan. My lease is up in a week or so. Instead of going month to month, I could move in with you.'

He held his breath and looked at me sideways.

Oh shit.

'Um...' I said. 'Um...'

'Forget I mentioned it,' he said quickly.

'No, no.' How could I explain? 'Um... living together would be lovely...but—you know what my parents are like.' Catholic. Very Catholic. Very disapproving of peole who 'lived in sin'.

'So?' He tried to grin. 'I don't want to live with them.'

'You have no idea what it would be like,' I said with difficulty. My heart was lodged in my larynx; I could barely speak. I *so* did not want this to hurt him or drive him away. 'They'd stop talking to me.'

'They wouldn't. They love you.'

'They never talked to my cousin Christine after she moved in with her boyfriend. None of them, aunts, uncles, cousins. No one. Not until Christine and Jeff got married.'

His look was a combination of surprise and disgust.

'That's medieval.'

I shrugged with one shoulder. 'They know what they believe and they stand up for it.'

'And you won't defy them.' That was a statement. His face was closed down, almost contemplative. I didn't want to think about what he might be contemplating.

I wanted to choose my words very carefully. It wasn't like we weren't having sex, after all. Most men would love this situation.

'If there was a good reason for it, I would stand up to them, like-'

He didn't let me finish.

'And I'm not a good enough reason.'

Then he stood up and walked out, past the life-size statue of Elvis and the big pink flamingo which guarded the door.

I grabbed my purse and ran after him.

It was so quiet outside the club, with only the noise of a train pulling into the nearby station. The sky was covered with clouds, and the streetlights cast clear circles of light on the footpath and road.

Tol stood with his back to me, under a light, his dark hair shining. I don't think he was waiting for me; more that he'd stopped to catch his breath—or his thoughts.

It was as though someone kicked me in the gut. I loved him so much. But life had been wonderful recently, and I knew my family would react...badly. And then Tol would go to Jordan, and there I'd be, without family or boyfriend.

It was a bleak prospect. I knew that he was right, I should be honest with them, but I wasn't sure I could cope with it all. I'd never *lied* to them. But, you know, they'd been very careful not to ask any questions, and I didn't know what to make of that. Maybe I was afraid to find out.

Walking quietly, speaking quietly, I went up behind him and said, 'We've had this discussion before. You want me to disrupt my relationship with my family, for the sake of a few weeks together, and then you'll leave, and you might never come back.'

The thought tore something inside me. He went very still, then turned around.

'I guess you'll have to decide whether this is long term or not.' I couldn't see his eyes, and his hands were jammed into his pockets. 'It's true I'm leaving, but I thought...'

What? *What?* It felt like I was the only one being asked to give up anything. He was jauntering off to Jordan, and he'd be gone for at least a year. He hadn't promised to come back. He hadn't even said he loved me.

'Never mind,' he said. 'I guess I was wrong.'

He turned away and walked towards the station, quickly. Numb, I watched him go.

I didn't call him back.

Instead, I got in my car and drove home. The first time that going back to my little house wasn't a delight.

———

WHEN I GOT HOME, alone, I had to do something to take my mind off Tol. I would have called him, but I didn't know what to say. A part of me wanted to say, 'My family would talk to us if we got married before you moved in.' Another part knew that was relationship suicide. Besides, I'd known Tol only a couple of months. Surely that wasn't long enough to decide that I wanted to marry him?

Was it?

Contemplating marriage is at least as scary as contemplating a break up.

I've always been good at not thinking about things. So I sat at my computer and researched the Mancuses.

It seemed to me that Melissa was unlikely to have believed the best of someone she'd never met, so the issue Jane had told her about was probably about someone she *had* met—through Jane. Most likely a Mancus or friend of one.

Mancus & Sons was still a private company. It had been started by Jane's great-great-grandfather, Alexander Mancus, who'd come here from Hawaii in the 1860s when the sugar trade started up in Queensland. He'd managed a mill in Hawaii and brought those skills to the fledgling industry—the Mancuses had never owned a sugar cane farm, only the milling and distri-bution networks. And the ships which took their product all over the world. And the rum production facilities which produced a world-famous brand. I'd had a few Mancus and

Cokes in my time, myself. It was more expensive than Bundy, but smoother. My mother used it every year for the Christmas cakes.

These days, Mancus & Sons were diversifying into green energy —cane waste is a surprisingly effective biofuel, although not great for climate change—and their beverage holdings included vineyards, a brewery, and a soft drink company. Wine coolers and canned mixed drinks were a big seller. They'd been one of the strongest opponents of the Federal Government's excise increase on pre-mixed drinks, and no wonder.

But there weren't any great scandals in the recent past.

In one old interview with William, I discovered that Jane's father, Frank, had retreated to the country to raise Red Angus cattle, a pursuit which seemed to fill his brother with bemused contempt. The obituary section of the Orange newspaper showed that Frank had died five years ago; Jane's mother, Winifred, last year, leaving only Jane behind. Both upstanding members of the community and, reading between the lines, actual nice people.

Jane's aunt, Susan, who had also lived with her family in Orange, had died some years ago without children, so William was the only one alive of his generation and the only Mancuses left were the ones in Sydney. I searched the telephone directory for their addresses, but of course they weren't listed. Jane's address book had only listed their phone numbers; of course she would have known where they lived.

So I searched gossip columns and gracious living magazines.

William Mancus, it turned out, had a spread out past Dural, in Arcadia, ten acres in prime horse-riding country. The house he and his wife, Margaret, had built had won seven separate awards. From the pictures, it was both hideous and huge, with big curving concrete walls—a sure-fire winner in Sydney's insane architecture scene. There was another article about the state-of-the-art security system and 24-hour guards. I realised that the address was the same one that Melissa had given me for Jane's grandmother, the matriarch of the family, Joanna Mancus. Very little had been written about her recently—the last trace was three years ago, a spread from the Black and White Ball, the biggest charity bash in Sydney's socialite calendar. Joanna Mancus was pictured as one of the organisers.

In the picture she looked old—a smiling little old lady. But the way the other, much younger, organisers were grouped around her and angled to stand next to her, she was no shrinking violet; more likely the top of the pecking order, which meant that she was a mover and shaker in the A-list social scene. A position of considerable power over those who cared about that sort of thing, and not a position one acquired simply with wealth. Joanna Mancus had to be a woman of some determination and strength.

William's wife, Margaret, was a 'home-maker' and everything written about her talked about her loving support of her family —but the images of her showed (underneath the perfect grooming and coifed blonde hair) a shrewd, closed-in face, which was unlikely to suffer fools gladly.

William's brother, Peter, was an 'entrepeneur'—a venture capitalist and ruthless property developer who had been photographed, I found, with a number of government ministers and the opposition leader's competition in the leadership spill, Murray Venati, he of the wandering hands and morals of a rattlesnake. Peter's wife, Samantha, was an A-list charitable high-flyer, notable only for the rigid perfection of her heavilybotoxed face. Their daughter, Paige, had started life as a pony club gymkhana girl but had graduated to clubbing, drinking, and getting photographed topless on Bondi beach. She claimed, according to the blog of a friend, to be studying social work because, 'I just want to give back' but I suspected that was more Daddy's PR machine at work than a social conscience.

All in all, it was hard to imagine a worse family for enthusiastic, honourable Jane.

Which made it interesting that the whole family lived together on the Dural property. It wasn't a direct line of travel from there to Galston Gorge, but it wasn't that far either.

I wondered how Paige, the clubbing cousin, managed her nightlife from Dural, which was a good hour's drive from the city. But almost certainly they had a *pied-à-terre* in town.

I wondered what Paige's parents would think if she moved in with *her* boyfriend. I called Tol. He didn't answer.

I went to bed and cried.

Chapter 11

Tuesday/Wednesday/Thursday

The wonderful thing about NewsCaff, I discovered, was that you never had time to think about personal problems. It started early, at home, with a conference call about the plan for the day, and then it went into overdrive.

My day was full—overfull—of story leads, stories which petered out, stories which might pay off in a week, stories which were being contradicted as I researched them.

Somehow, without a word being said, I had graduated from soft stories to hard news.

The other wonderful thing, I found out at lunchtime, was that journalists and researchers love to talk about the stories they can't run.

I heard all about Paige Mancus's cocaine habit, Peter Mancus's shady property deals, his wife Samantha's gambling problem. The stories weren't 'news' so the information was little more than gossip—but it cast a light, nonetheless. Nothing about William and Margaret, though.

'*Squeaky* clean, kid,' Jack said, leaning back in his chair, balancing a plastic tray of sushi on his chest. 'The very proper upright gentleman, is William.'

'And Margaret?' I asked, sipping coffee. I didn't have much of an appetite; my stomach had been tied in knots all day.

Claudia made a face. 'She took over from the old lady—runs several charities with an iron fist—but they do good work and they're a lot more efficient than most NGOs.'

'Which ones?'

'Trusts the family endowed: um, the Settler Foundation, the Mancus Charitable Organisation, and my personal favourite, the Deserving Poor Foundation.'

'You're kidding!'

She laughed like a drain. 'They don't call it that any more, of course, Now it's the No Limit Foundation. But it was incorporated in the 19th century, and its legal name is still Deserving Poor!'

I thought, inevitably, of the speech Liza Dootlittle's father makes in *My Fair Lady*, where he admits he belongs to the Undeserving Poor: 'I don't eat any less than a deserving man, and I drinks a good deal more!' I'd always had a bit of sympathy for that position.

'Not exactly PC,' I said.

Jack grinned. 'Times change.'

I finished my coffee and got up to wash it out in the kitchenette, which abutted the office.

'Seems like one of those charities would be more of a natural home for Jane than NewsCaff.'

'Are you kidding?' Claudia said. 'To run a charity you have to be tough as nails—too much empathy and you go under, not to mention being taken advantage of by every con man and grifter in the target group. Jane wouldn't have lasted a week.'

But still, as I went back to setting up a phone interview with a Russian dissident in hiding in Georgia, somehow the idea of Jane and charity work wouldn't go away.

———

ON A CLOUDLESS SUMMER evening in Sydney, the sky takes on a purple shade just after the sun sets. And then the fruit bats fly over, heading for the Moreton Bay figs by the Harbour, taking your eyes up to just-emerging stars. The air smells of heat and jasmine and car fumes, and your feet stick slightly to the still-warm asphalt as you cross the road.

I walked up my street more slowly than normal, hoping against hope that Tol would be there to greet me as he'd been the night before. But there were no lights on. My gut clenched tight again. I felt sick.

Not knowing if I should ring him or not, I opened my door, bending to pick up the letters on the mat inside. As I straightened, something hit me from behind. I fell forward, and felt a foot in my backside push me hard to the floor. I tried to twist, to get my hands up to defend myself, but a heavy shoe came down on my back. I smelt something. Earl Grey tea? Bergamot. Then someone dragged letters out from under me, and then they hit me on the head again, and ran.

I didn't quite pass out, although the light darkened around me and my head felt like it was split in half. The room spun, I couldn't get my legs under me to stand up, I felt sick. Shaking. When I tried to lift my head, I vomited. The smell made my head worse.

Keeping my head as still as possible, I groped for my bag and fished out my phone. Tol. His number was at the top of my favourites list. I touched it, smearing a trace of puke on the screen. It made me want to cry. I couldn't lift the phone to my ear somehow, so I touched the speaker icon. Please answer. Please.

'Poppy, I'm not sure-'

'Tol. I. Oh god. Someone hit me.' I was crying like a kid.

'Where are you?' His voice was tight with worry.

'At home.'

'I'll be right there, sweetheart. Do you want me to call an ambulance?'

'I don't know,' I wailed. I'd never felt like this before; out of control, helpless, useless.

'Sit tight. Don't hang up.' As he spoke I heard a door slam, his footsteps running. He panted as he ran. 'Keep talking to me.'

'I can't talk. I feel sick. I-I puked all over the floor!'

He swore. 'Sweetheart, I'm going to put you on hold while I call an ambulance, okay?'

'Okay,' I said, my voice sounding very small and shaky.

I tried to sit up, but I retched again, so I inched back from the puke and lay down on the cool wooden floor. That felt better.

Maybe I could have a nap. Except you weren't supposed to sleep after a concussion, were you?

The light was so bright; spots of it were dancing in front of me. I'd just close my eyes. That couldn't hurt.

Tol's voice came from somewhere close and I thought blearily that the phone reception was really good.

'Poppy! Poppy, wake up, sweetheart! Talk to me.'

Tol wanted me to talk to him. That was nice. I smiled muzzily and said, 'Tol,' without opening my eyes.

'Poppy! Talk to me.'

'I love you, Tolly,' I said. His hand was on my face, and I nuzzled into it. I heard him sigh.

'Open your eyes, Poppy,' he said.

I opened my eyes with difficulty. His face was blurry, as though I needed glasses to see him properly.

'Hello,' I said.

'Hello,' he said. He stroked the hair back from my head. I could hear a siren approaching. 'The ambulance is coming. What happened?'

'Someone stole my letters.'

'Your letters?'

I tried to remember what I'd told Tol about Jane and Melissa. But I couldn't.

'Never mind,' Tol said. 'Here're the paramedics.'

Then the nice ambulance people came and gave me an ice pack for my head and took me to hospital. My parents turned up fifteen minutes later and insisted on staying until I was admitted to a ward. They smiled approvingly at Tol and worriedly at me and it was a relief when, three hours later, I was wheeled up to a ward for overnight observation, and they went home. Tol stayed, paying no attention at all to the scheduled visiting hours. By then, the three-inch gash on my head had been stitched and I had been given excellent painkillers and decided that I loved the entire medical profession.

Having been informed by the hospital that I had been assaulted, some police officers came to take my statement.

Between concussion and painkillers, I don't think I was very coherent, but they seemed to get the gist of it all, although the female constable (Constable Nguyen) didn't look too convinced by my ramblings.

'Better call Detective Chloe,' I said finally.

'Chloe Prudhomme in Major Crimes,' Tol added helpfully.

Constable Nguyen sniffed. 'Assault like this isn't a Major Crime.'

'*If* you had been listening,' Tol said, a dangerous note in his voice, 'you would have realised that the letters which were stolen contained evidence in a homicide and possible kidnapping.'

The two police officers exchanged glances and shrugged.

'We'll send a memo,' Constable Nguyen said. 'Major Crime don't like it much when we lowly plods put our oar in.'

'Fine!' Tol snapped. 'I'll call her myself.'

'Sign here,' Nguyen said to me, proffering a crime report form and a pen. I signed, shakily.

Tol was calling Detective Chloe, using my phone which he had thoughtfully wiped free of puke. At my insistence, he also called Tyler and kept him in the loop.

And an hour later I had to go through it all again for Detectives Chloe and Martin.

'Why would this have anything to do with Jane and Melissa?' I asked peevishly.

'Because whoever it was didn't take your purse, they took your letters,' Detective Chloe said.

Which made no sense to me at all, or to them.

By the time it was all over, it was after midnight. Just as well I wasn't allowed to go to sleep.

Chloe and Martin left; Tol was sprawled in a chair next to my bed. I was in a four-bed room and the curtains were drawn around us, but we could hear various monitors beeping and the eternal hiss of the air conditioner. The woman in the next bed was snoring loudly.

I stared down at Tol; he stared back, straightening and getting up to sit on the bed so that our faces were on a level. He touched my cheek, just as he had before the ambulance came.

'Thank you for rescuing me,' I said.

'You said you loved me.'

I winced, involuntarily, remembering how horrible I must have looked, and he moved back a little, his eyes showing hurt. No nonono. I grabbed his hand and held tight.

'Not the most romantic declaration. No sexy dress, no high heels or make up. It would have been nice if I'd been upright, at least.' I tried to make light of it, but my heart kept climbing up into my throat, trying to choke me.

He ignored the babbling, his eyes serious.

'You said you loved me.'

'Yes. That's what I said.'

Nodding slowly, he raised my hand to his lips and kissed my knuckles very gently.

'Okay. Okay. That's good.'

I waited. Everyone knew how this was supposed to go, right. I say I love you, you say you love me. Otherwise, things were *not* good.

'Just one thing,' he said, a gleam of humour in his eyes. 'Don't call me Tolly, all right? Or it's all over.'

My eyes filled with tears. I felt so *weak*, dammit, and it wasn't just the concussion or the shock of being attacked. Everything about him unmanned me. Unwomanned me.

'Oh, sweetheart, don't cry.' He slid further up the bed and put his arm around my shoulders. 'I was only teasing.'

I hiccuped into his shoulder, 'Don't tease me. I'm *sick*.'

'Poor baby. Poor little one. You know I love you, right? You know I do.'

Tears in my eyes, I blinked at him. 'Really?'

His mouth touched mine gently, featherlight.

'Very truly really.'

'O-kay.' I sniffed and fumbled for a tissue, which Tol got out of the box and handed to me. Just my luck to need to blow my nose loudly in the middle of the most romantic conversation I would probably ever have.

'Move over,' Tol said.

He lay down beside me and pulled my head gently onto his shoulder.

'There we go, my love. But don't go to sleep.'

'Okay.'

I couldn't seem to say anything except okay. I made an effort to concentrate.

'I do very truly really love you, too.'

There. That was how it was supposed to work. Happiness bloomed inside me.

Tol kissed my forehead, lips warm and real.

'That's my girl,' he said.

———

THEY LET me go to sleep around three am, and then woke me at six to ask if I wanted a cup of tea. Argh.

At ten they let me go home. Tol offered to take the day off work, but what were retired parents for? So Mum and Dad picked me up and took me back to their place where I slept the rest of the day away and woke up at dinner time famished and headachy, but otherwise okay.

I couldn't help smiling every time I thought of Tol. But there were more serious things to think about. Like—who had hit me, and what had been in that letter?

What the hell, I thought. I still had Melissa's home number in my phone, so before I went downstairs to face the barrage of questions from my family, I rang her husband.

'Tim Hunter,' he answered. He sounded tired.

I explained who I was, and he remembered me calling before. 'Mr Hunter, someone attacked me last night and took my letters.'

'Christ,' he said, shaken. 'The letter Melissa sent you?'

'She sent me a letter?' I yelped and then clutched my head as pain lanced through it.

'From the Menzies. She spoke to me about an hour after she'd got in, and she said she'd tell me all about it when she got home, but she mentioned she'd sent you a letter explaining everything.'

'Do you know what "everything" meant?'

'I don't know anything solid,' he said.

He was a farmer, the type of man who wouldn't want to say anything that wasn't 'solid'. But my pounding head made me impatient with that nicety, and I said so.

Silence for a moment.

'It might have had something to do with Jane's family,' he said slowly. 'Because they invited her to stay with them for the funeral, but when I said that was a good idea, she got this funny look on her face and shook her head.'

'They invited her? Who?'

'Jane's grandma, Joanna. Melissa and Jane used to stay with her on long weekends from boarding school, you know. Joanna always liked Melissa. She came to our wedding. Gave us a Christofle cutlery set.' His voice broke. 'The police won't tell me anything! Do *you* think she's dead?'

I was silent for a moment.

'Whatever this secret was, someone killed Jane for it,' I said eventually. 'And they almost killed me.'

I heard a despairing sob, then he hung up.

Poor bastard. I touched the lump on my head and was filled with righteous anger towards whoever was behind all of this.

Ringing Detective Chloe took all my concentration. My eyes didn't seem to be working quite right, but I thought that was because of the painkillers rather than the concussion.

'Prudhomme.'

I told her about Melissa sending me a letter.

'Hmm. Well, that explains the attack. Bugger. This bastard's a step ahead of us.'

She hung up without asking how I was. Charming.

Something tugged at the back of my mind; something Tim Hunter had said. Christofle cutlery set. That would have cost thousands. Money. That was what was tugging at me. Follow the money.

As I tottered downstairs, feeling rather more woozy than I had expected, I considered what I knew about the Mancus company.

There had been four people in William's generation. Two of them were dead. Jane, no doubt, had inherited her father's portion of shares. Her aunt was also dead, and she had lived with Jane's family. Was it too great a reach to assume that Jane had inherited her share as well? And, if so, had that given Jane control of the company?

How would I find that out?

After dinner, where my sister-in-law Bernadette berated me for being so stupid as to get involved 'in what are clearly some very shady activities' and thereby bringing shame on the family until my father said, 'That's enough, Bernie,' in his no-nonsense voice, I retreated to my own house.

'I'm fine,' I insisted, but even if I hadn't been I would have run away from the disapproval and barely restrained curiosity around the table. That's the disadvantage of a big family. At that moment, Bernadette never speaking to me again if Tol moved in wasn't sounding so bad

Dad walked me home to make sure I got there safely this time. I was a bit surprised that he and Mum hadn't made more objections to me leaving.

'You're sure you're all right?' he asked as we neared my gate.

'Course I am.'

'You don't want one of us with you?'

'They got what they came for, Dad. They won't be back.'

He humphed. 'Maybe. I- uh—I called Tol. He says he can come over and sleep on the couch.'

I just stared at him.

'That's all right, isn't it? You trust him?'

'Yes, of course I trust him!'

Nodding with satisfaction, he took my key and led me in the gate, leaving me flabbergasted. They must *really* like Tol.

I shook a little as I looked at the front step of my little house, but I kept it from Dad as he opened the door, went in first and looked around, and only then let me go in. I smiled at him. He was still a strong, well-set up man—years of wrestling beef carcasses had left him with muscles and hands like hams. But his hair had almost completely retreated and what there was, was grey. Yet he was sure he could protect me. It made me want to cry, which was probably a good sign that I wasn't fully recovered yet. He kissed my cheek and patted me awkwardly on the back.

'Go to bed,' he said. 'Tol's coming right after his Uni class. He should be here in half an hour or so. I'll stay until then.'

As I closed the door and dragged myself up the stairs, I laughed at the irony of my father *asking* my boyfriend to spend the night.

But then, instead of going to bed as I no doubt ought to considering the thundering headache I had, I googled for instructions on how to find Jane's will. Turned out I had to put a form in at the Supreme Court of NSW and pay a fairly hefty fee.

I printed out the form, but I ran out of energy and left it in the print tray. Surely Chloe would follow the money too?

That was what Tol said when he got there. I heard him come in and talk quietly with my father, then Dad called, 'Bye, now,' and the front door closed. Tol bounded up the stairs and into my bedroom, looking rather pleased with himself.

'I told your father I would stay here until all this was cleared up,' he announced. 'He thanked me profusely.'

I laughed, and he grinned at me.

'So now I can answer the phone any time of the day or night,' he said with smug satisfaction. Then he sobered. 'But we're going to have to talk at some point.'

Damn. I knew it was too good to last. It all just seemed overwhelming right then...tears started to scald my eyes.

Hastily, Tol hugged me.

'Don't worry now. Maybe this will never get cleared up and I'll get to stay here until I leave.'

That sounded good. But...I blinked the tears back and frowned. 'I want this bastard locked up,' I said, touching my head gingerly. Tol's face clouded and his eyes flashed with anger.

'Yes,' was all he said, but he meant it.

And the funny thing was, he slept on the couch after all, because my head was so sore I couldn't bear to be touched.

———

Thursday

The doctor had told me not to go back to work for a couple of days, but Barry was on the phone to me first thing, begging me to at least do some phone and internet work from home. So I did, because it stopped my mind replaying that horrible moment when I was hit and immobilised. It was worse in retrospect; I shook with the memory of helplessness and pain.

By lunchtime, I had relived it often enough to get past the horror and make it safely back to anger. So I called Detective Chloe again.

'No, I don't have any more information for you,' she said as soon as she answered.

So much for good manners. I replied in kind. 'Who inherits from Jane and did she have control of the company?'

There was a brief silence, and then a sigh. A long-suffering sigh.

'We haven't tracked her will down yet and no one will answer any questions about her financial status until we get a subpoena. We're waiting on the police prosecutor.'

'How long will that take?'

She sniffed. 'This is the Mancuses. The prosecutor wants to be 110% sure of his legal ground.'

'Surely it's routine to look at the financials of a murder victim?'

'You'd think so,' Chloe said dryly.

'Has anyone talked to Joanna?'

'Who?'

'The grandmother. She was close to Jane, apparently.'

'None of the family are prepared to talk to us. And we don't have any evidence which might let us compel them. Hell, for all we know Jane met someone at a bar and had her drink spiked.'

'Hah!' I said. What the hell. In for a penny. 'I bet Tim Hunter could get you in. Or maybe me.'

I left it hanging.

'Given that you only just came out of the last episode alive, I wouldn't have thought you would want to put yourself in harm's way again,' Chloe said slowly.

'By talking to a little old lady?'

'I want *every* detail,' she said fiercely. 'Every single fucking detail. Use that ridiculous talent of yours for getting people to tell you things they'd never tell anyone else. And write it all down afterwards before you forget anything.'

Heavens to Betsy. Clearly Detective Chloe didn't like being stonewalled by a bunch of silvertails. Which was kind of funny, because her family were fairly silver-tailed themselves.

'Yes, ma'am!' I said.

'All right.' She hung up. I stared at the phone and slowly grinned. I had permission to go and be as nosy as I liked.

I just had to get into one of the most tightly secured private homes in Australia.

Chapter 12

Thursday/Friday

Tim Hunter was more than happy to ring Joanna for me and set up a meeting. I think he was relieved to have something concrete to do.

'I'll tell her you need to discuss Jane's work,' he said. That seemed pretty thin to me, but sure enough, a few minutes later he texted me Joanna's phone number and a time for me to be at the 'estate' the next morning.

So once the working day was over I settled in for some serious research on Joanna Mancus in order to decide what to wear. It was vital that I looked like someone she could trust.

Apart from to the Black and White Ball-type functions, Joanna Mancus wore suits. Chanel suits. I had as much chance of getting a Chanel suit as of being elected Prime Minister—but fortunately, that style is the single most copied fashion item in existence, and my sister Theresa is an aficionado. I called her. She brought over four suits and fifteen blouses (Theresa is a solicitor, in a firm where this kind of dressing is mandatory). We settled, after some discussion, on a French navy silk twill with an off-white shell and navy court shoes. We worked out a way of doing my hair which covered up the stitches, and she laid down the law about how much and what kind of make-up I should use.

She had to go out and buy me some unladdered pantyhose, but after that she left in a glow of self-satisfaction and the unexpressed but clear hope that finally I'd come to my senses and decided to 'make the most of myself', as she had been urging me to for years. Don't get the wrong idea. Theresa is, at heart, a lovely person. But her values and mine are a long way apart. She's very... respectable.

The next morning, my slightly aching head and I were driving sedately down the road in Dural which led to the Mancus house. It was lined on both sides with very expensive real estate, so I drove between high brick walls with iron spikes on the top. Past security cameras which pointed both inside and outside the estates. And, finally, to the double wrought iron gates complete with one of those little guard houses at the side that you get in military installations. The guard checked my name and my drivers' licence, then waved me through. The gates looked as though they dated back to the 19th century, but they swung open and closed behind my old Corolla soundlessly.

The drive wound up through two rows of old palm trees. Beyond the trees, lawns stretched, lush and green; there were massed plantings of roses in curved beds. Within this conventional landscape the house sat like an alien invader, the kind of house where you'd expect cyborgs to live. I knew that William had torn down the house his grandfather had built in order to construct this monstrosity. I wondered how Joanna Mancus, who liked Chanel suits, felt about it.

I parked to the side of the circular drive and walked towards the double doors—some kind of hardwood, like Sydney redgum, I thought, which glowed a rich ruby in the morning light. They were asymmetric; the left hand one came to a point on one side, the right hand one was straight. It was oddly disconcerting.

The right door opened as I approached, held by a thirty-some-thing dark-haired woman dressed in a pair of black tailored trousers, a white short-sleeved blouse and flat black pumps. Her hair was caught back in a sleek ponytail and her eyes were outlined delicately in kohl. Middle Eastern? I wondered. Or perhaps Greek.

'Ms McGowan,' she stated. I nodded. She stepped back without introducing herself and ushered me in.

'And you are?' I said brightly.

She blinked. Perhaps proper guests didn't ask the name of the help.

'Angela,' she said. 'Come this way.'

The front hall had an asymmetric ceiling which echoed the shape of the doors. It rose to a blazing height, clerestory windows flooding the area with light—actually, more like glare than light at this hour.

The walls were brushed concrete. Actual concrete. And the floors were polished concrete. I was astounded, yet again, at the ugliness really rich people were prepared to live with. If I had their money...

Angela led the way down a long corridor. On one side a glass wall showed a tropical rainforest—so dense I couldn't see the other side. On the other side, a gallery-style wall of art. I recognised a number of famous Australian artists: Blackman, Williams, Olsen, even a classic Brett Whitely from the Sydney Harbour series. The white sails of the Opera House were echoed in the bellied spinnakers of yachts racing past Fort Denison. The whole thing was alive with joy and the salt scent of the sea. At least they had good taste in art.

The corridor opened into a... realtors would call it a 'reception room', I guess. It was huge, furnished in the minimalist style of low leather and chrome, the whole thing built around the wall to floor doors—again, asymmetric—which led out onto a terrace with a cactus garden separating the terrace from the rolling grounds beyond. It was impressive, expensive, and as homely as an airport.

Another corridor, with me trying not to make too much noise in my unaccustomed heels on the bare concrete.

Another redgum door.

Beyond, a different world.

This room was large, but it was human-sized, divided into two usable areas of chintz-covered lounge chairs around a fireplace and an office space with a beautiful rosewood desk and floor to ceiling bookshelves. Wooden floors, with Chinese rugs. The walls were plastered, with cornices and ceilings at a comfortable height. I could feel myself relaxing as I took in the warm reds and golds of the colour scheme. The side tables and cabinets were antiques in a mix of styles, united by glowing wood and gentle curves.

A woman rose to greet me from the chair nearest the fireplace. Joanna Mancus. My height, but clearly reduced from being taller in her youth. Very pretty, even now, with pure white hair carefully waved, and discreet makeup. Dressed as Angela had been in dark slacks and a silk blouse. I thought for a moment that I'd made a terrible mistake about the suit, but then I saw her blue eyes give that flick up and down that women do who care about clothes, and her mouth relaxed fractionally as she held out her hand.

'Miss McGowan,' she said, smiling. Her voice was warmer than I'd expected, and I realised that the photos online had given no clue to her real power: that of charm.

'Mrs Mancus,' I replied. 'Thank you for seeing me.'

She waved me to a seat and nodded to Angela, who disappeared through a door on the other side of the room.

'I have my own little kitchen,' Mrs Mancus said. 'Angela will make us tea. I hope that's all right?' I realised I had segued from thinking of her as Joanna to thinking of her as Mrs Mancus.

'Of course,' I said. 'Lovely.' I sat up straight on the chair, as she was doing. Just like my nanna used to tell me to.

'Tim tells me you worked with Jane?' she probed, delicately.

'Not exactly. I've taken over her job temporarily, until they find a replacement.' She stiffened, just a little, so I added, 'I work in the Children's Department normally.' As I expected, she relaxed. There's something so respectable and non-threatening about working for children.

'And you asked to see me because?'

I'd practised this moment all the way in the car.

'Mrs Mancus, the police are asking us for Jane's records. The head of News and Current Affairs doesn't want to give them— you know, protecting the freedom of the press and all that.' She nodded, but she was holding back any encouragement. 'The problem we have is that the police don't actually understand why Jane was driving on that road at all that day. If she was going to the site her calendar said, she should have come to Galston Gorge from the other direction. And the police won't give up on getting her records because they think she was out there for some other purpose.'

'I'm sorry, Miss McGowan, but I don't quite understand what I can do-?'

'Do you know where Jane was the morning of the accident? If we could verify that she was on that road on ABC business— that is, that she was heading to the recce site from another place —then we could refuse to give the police the records. Which include all her diaries and emails.'

She stilled, those clear blue eyes studying me narrowly. Was I being too obvious?

'You think she was here,' Mrs Mancus said. How much to say? At least I was sure that Mrs Mancus wasn't the one who attacked me. She didn't have the physical heft of whoever had put their boot in my back. But she had more than enough money to pay someone hefty.

I shrugged, delicately. 'Visiting family? It had occurred to me.'

She turned her head, staring into the fireplace, where the grate had been filled with an elaborate flower arrangement; roses and lilies scenting the air. The faint smell of ash lay underneath.

She cleared her throat gently.

'Melissa Hunter is missing,' she said.

'Yes.'

'I remember her as a schoolgirl. She and Jane were a pair—so... so *country*.' I couldn't tell if 'country' was a compliment or an insult. 'Jane always believed the best of everyone.' Her hands, which had lain quietly in her lap, tightened until the knuckles were white.

Breaking into this reminiscence would have been crass. I sat in respectful silence.

'Do you think Melissa is dead?' she asked harshly, turning her head like a snake striking. The charm was gone, and the intellect behind it blazed out.

'Yes,' I said.

'Do you think the same person killed Jane?'

'Yes.'

She nodded. 'And you're not really here because the police want Jane's records, are you?'

How much to tell her? My instinct is to tell the truth, but Joanna Mancus had given absolutely nothing away so far. She had been more controlled than I quite liked. But she was no fool, and I suspected that if she wanted to kill someone she would have done so with a lot more finesse than spiking a drink with speed. In fact, if Joanna Mancus killed someone, I doubted anyone would ever realise it had been murder.

There's a part of me which respects competence. I reached up and parted my hair so she could see the stitches.

'That was all true. But Melissa wrote me a letter telling me a secret Jane had shared with her. Someone attacked me and took that letter before I had a chance to read it. To tell you the truth, I'd like to see that person behind bars.'

'Ah. Yes, I understand that.'

Angela came back, carrying a tray with tea, little friands and tiny triangular sandwiches. We busied ourselves with the ritual and sipped genteelly in silence for a moment. The sandwiches were chicken salad, and delicious.

'I did not see Jane that morning,' she said, putting the fragile china cup back on the saucer with deliberation.

'But?'

'There are no "buts", Miss McGowan. I cannot help you in that regard.'

Which left open the possibility of her helping me in other regards. We locked gazes, and I nodded.

'Did Jane inherit her father's estate? And her aunt's?'

A small smile tugged at her mouth. 'Jane, my dear, owned exactly 50% of Mancus & Sons. And before you ask—I own 25% and my son, William, owns the rest.'

'And Peter...'

A shadow went over her face. 'My husband's will was made before Peter was born. Foolishly, he never changed it. Thought he would live forever, I daresay. He was a very vital man.'

'That must have made Peter...unhappy.'

'Oh, no. The others combined with me to give Peter a suitable financial inheritance.' No shares, though. They didn't let go of a single share. If I were Peter, I'd feel shut out and infantilised. As the youngest child, I knew that feeling. Your older siblings often had no confidence that you could be competent at anything.

Mrs Mancus continued.

'But Jane was quite happy to allow William to continue as the CEO. She was set on a career as a news broadcaster, although of course there was no need for her to work at all.'

'Mrs Mancus, I'm trying to understand what kind of person Jane was.'

Angela came back and began to pack up the tray. Mrs Mancus gazed at her meditatively, but I didn't think she was seeing Angela.

'She liked horses. She understood horses better than she understood people,' she said. There was a note in her voice—sadness? Regret? Or contempt?

'You keep horses here?'

'Just a pony or two; Paige doesn't ride any more.'

'Were Paige and Jane close? Horses bringing them together?'

A flicker of contempt went over her face. 'As I said, Paige doesn't ride any more.' She stood up and perforce I stood with her.

She gestured with the economy of movement of someone with arthritis. 'Angela will show you out.'

Before I left, I looked her in the eye. 'Two people are dead, Mrs Mancus. Two women you knew. One of them was your granddaughter. Aren't you at all curious?'

An expression flickered over her face and was gone.

'I've seen a lot of people die, Miss McGowan.'

'Who gets Jane's share of the company now?'

She smiled, wryly. 'I do. Thank you, Angela.'

I followed Angela's straight back and shining ponytail down the long corridor to the front door. In the huge reception room a woman was on the phone. Margaret Mancus, William's wife. She was in a lilac lounging suit—it would have been sacrilege to call them sweats, since clearly she'd never sweated in them. She was ordering catering for some event, and she was very, very picky.

'No, no, I want rock lobster from southern Tasmania, not Perth, they are never fresh enough when they come in from WA-' She broke off as we walked through and examined me.

'Who are you?' she demanded, ignoring the voice coming from the handset.

'I'm Poppy McGowan. I've just been chatting with Joanna about Jane.'

I felt a little shabby about claiming first name basis with Mrs Mancus, but it worked. Margaret Mancus blinked and reassessed me.

'You were a friend of hers?'

'I work at the ABC. I'm a researcher with the Daily Report.' True, all true. Not my fault if she was misled.

'A terrible thing,' she said briskly. 'We were all shocked. I never even knew that Jane drank.'

'She didn't. Her soft drink was spiked.'

That shocked her. In reflex, she pushed back her blond hair from her forehead with the back of her hand, still holding the phone.

'You didn't know?' I asked.

'The newspapers said-'

'The police didn't tell you?'

She waved her free hand and pushed her hair back again with the phone, but she didn't seem to realise she was holding it. She'd certainly forgotten her call.

'Oh, William wouldn't allow the police to question *me*,' she said, as if that were the most normal thing in the world, as if it were natural for a man to protect her from all unpleasantness— and to have the power to do so. Then, as if to herself, 'Who on earth would do such a thing?' She stared at the phone and seemed to remember what she'd been doing. 'I'm so sorry, Misser—I'm in the middle of organising an event for the No Limits Foundation at the moment. Perhaps-' She gazed vaguely at Angela, and even though I didn't know her, I could see that the vagueness was unusual in her from Angela's suddenly sharpened look. 'Give Miss er my card, Angela.' She nodded to me. 'If you find out anything more, give me a call, won't you?' Then she turned her back and took up exactly where she'd left off. 'Not fresh enough, yes, that's what I said.'

Angela walked on, and I followed her. That had been a very odd little encounter. It was hard to get a fix on Margaret Mancus— both precise and vague, businesslike and childlike.

Angela paused by a side table in the hall and handed me a card from a pile in a little silver dish. It said simply 'Margaret

Mancus' and a mobile number. Thick stock, raised lettering. How nice.

'Thank you,' I said. I followed her to the door. This was my only chance to talk to her. In all the Raymond Chandler books, the loyal servant would tip the wink to the PI in order to protect their old employer. I turned on the threshold. 'Angela, did you see Jane-'

She smiled and closed the door gently in my face.

Chapter 13

Friday

I called Detective Chloe, as promised, and repeated word for word everything that Joanna and I had said.

'Huh,' she said at the end. 'Okay. If you find out anything else, let me know.'

She was about to hang up.

'One thing,' I said. 'The Mancus's security cameras point outwards as well as inwards.'

'They won't give us the footage and no judge will give me a subpoena on the evidence we've got.'

'True,' I said cheerfully. 'But all their neighbours have the same security set-up. I'd be very surprised if you couldn't find someone along that road that wouldn't like to put the boot into the Mancuses. Particularly if you guarantee confidentiality.'

'Hmph. Maybe.'

That was it. How rude.

I thought of the elaborate formality of Joanna Mancus's tea ceremony; good manners taken to the extreme. But surely there was a middle ground where people could be a *little* polite?

After that, I decided I was well enough to go in to work. Maybe well enough that Tol wouldn't have to sleep on the couch tonight.

Barry greeted me with real enthusiasm and put me onto a story about a series of drive-by shootings within the Vietnamese community. I set up interviews with a Vietnamese MP, the local Police Commander from Cabramatta where the shootings had taken place, and got a phone interview from the brother of one of the victims. The brother was in Vietnam and had no intention of coming back anytime soon. He wasn't prepared to do a video interview, and there wasn't a reporter available, so I ended up taping our conversation then and there (with his permission, of course). We could use his Facebook picture to run the audio over.

We talked for a little while about his brother and what a wonderful person he'd been, how he'd been a perfect example of how a refugee family can make good in Australia. I didn't believe any of it. He sounded furious rather than grief-stricken. So I probed that anger.

'Some members of the community are saying your brother provoked the attack.'

'No fucking way! It's all about family power struggles,' he said in a broad Aussie accent. Like his brother, he'd been born here and considered himself Australian. 'The old people want things to run like they did in their day, but times have changed.

They're trying to take back the power from our generation but it's way too late for that.'

It all sounded very convincing unless you knew that the 'power' he was talking about was the distribution of heroin in Sydney, and the 'old people' were his two uncles, who'd run that trade for thirty years.

'Are you afraid to come back?' I asked.

'I'll come back in my own good time. And then those bastards had better watch out. That's all I've got to say.'

'Thanks for talking to us.'

'At least you treat me like a real person. The rest of those bloody reporters act like I'm a serial killer.'

'Can we get back to you if anything else happens?'

'Sure, love.' A suggestive note entered his voice. 'Anytime, anytime at all. As long as it's you.'

I played the conversation back to Barry and Jack, who looked at me with astonishment.

'How the hell did you get his number?' Jack asked. 'Every reporter in Australia's been trying to track him down.'

'His cousin makes traditional wedding gowns for Vietnamese girls; I did a story on it for *Launchpad* two years ago. So I rang her. She didn't want to make a statement herself, but she gave me Yien's number.'

'And he *talked* to you?'

'Sure,' I said, surprised. 'I told him that if he wanted to send a message to the people who killed his brother, the best way was by TV.'

'But he *talked* to you,' Jack repeated.

'People talk to me.' I shrugged. 'It just happens.'

'Bloody beauty,' Barry said. 'Tyler's going to eat my shit to get this.'

Ah, the wonderful world of television.

On my way home through the newly fallen night, I followed the trail of red tail lights across the Anzac Bridge and home to Annandale, thinking about old people trying to take back the power from the young by killing them. Fifty percent of a major Australian company was a lot of power. And Joanna was in her eighties, at least. If, on her death, her 25% was split up between her children and their children, that would have given Jane control.

Worth killing for?

On the other hand, Joanna now had complete control; 75% of the company. I very much doubted that William wanted his mother to have that much power—of course, I hadn't seen them together. Perhaps she was more than happy to let him run things his way.

I wondered who actually owned that house. The company? Joanna had made her own domain, but Margaret was the chatelaine, I thought. Joanna had definitely relished the fact that she had inherited Jane's shares. I could imagine her enjoying a situation which reversed the power in the house: where she had lived there at William's pleasure, now he was there at hers.

She wouldn't have been human if she hadn't found some satisfaction in that. Which was a far cry from killing Jane to get it.

I sighed as I parked my car outside my little house. I was sick of violence and death. Sick of people who wanted power. Sick of people who were prepared to kill others to get it. Whether it was the Nguyen uncles or one of the Mancuses, I was over them all.

I would stay out of it, I decided as I got out and opened my front door. I'd do my job until Barry and Tyler found a replacement, then I'd return to CHED and forget all about death and violence.

There was a card from the post office on my mat saying I had a registered letter to collect the next day. Oh, good. Before Tol had heard about the delay in his employment in Jordan, I'd planned to visit Tol on his dig there. A friend of my Aunty Mary, for various complicated reasons, had paid for me to have a first class ticket. Now we weren't going—or, at least, not *yet*—I had filled in all the forms to get the refund, which the friend had insisted I keep. This letter must be the cheque. Tol was home, cooking a tangy pasta sauce.

As we ate, we discussed all the things we could use the money for. There was still a lot to be done to the house; the bathroom, in particular, could use some work. It was a very domestic, happy conversation, and it made me seriously think about braving my parents' pain and let Tol move in. Even if it were only for a couple of months. Maybe if I went to confession after he'd left, they'd get over it.

'It would be good to have a higher shower head over the bath,' he said. 'I have to crouch down to get under the spray.'

'Poor tall person.' I grinned at him. 'We can do that, but you know how hard it is to get a plumber. By the time one arrives, you'll be in Jordan.'

I was just making a light-hearted comment, but he frowned.

'It's hard to imagine being there,' he said slowly. 'Hard to imagine being away from you.'

He didn't sleep on the couch that night. But I lay awake for a while, because it was all too easy for me to imagine him gone.

———

SATURDAY

Fortunately, the post office which services my area is open on Saturday morning. Tol and I picked up the registered letter with happy anticipation. There's nothing like unearned money to set your mood skyrocketing. Ripping it open as I walked out, I pulled out a letter. Not a business envelope, but a private one. The address on the back was Melissa Hunter's.

For a long moment I stood frozen in the doorway, the post office customers edging past me. Tol came up behind me.

'Poppy?'

Mutely, I showed him the envelope.

'We need coffee,' he said, and steered me down the road to Graziella's coffee bar. It was always busy on the weekend, but we found a table outside in the courtyard and sat under a green web of ornamental grape.

'I'll get coffee,' Tol said. 'Don't open it 'til I get back.' I nodded, still staring at the thick cream paper of the envelope, where Melissa's broad, sloping letters spelt out my name.

I couldn't get a hold on what I was feeling—just that it was very strong; a tumult of emotion. I was sure in my gut that this was a message from beyond the grave. Melissa Hunter was almost certainly dead. Whoever had attacked me didn't have it. I could find out what all this was about. But part of me—the part which had decided last night that I didn't want anything more to do with death and violence—didn't want to open it. It was repugnant, this expensive bit of stationery. Whatever was in it had caused two women's deaths. I felt as though I would be tainted by opening it.

When Tol came back with the cappuccinos, I was still staring at it.

'You don't have to open it,' he said, reading my mind as he so often did. 'You can just hand it over to Chloe.'

Oh, part of me wanted to do that. But I owed it to Melissa. She had written this to *me*, not to Chloe. I split the thick paper along the spine with my thumb and pulled out a single sheet of notepaper, written on with real ink from a fountain pen. Tol read over my shoulder.

'Dear Poppy,

I'm sure I'm over-reacting but I feel safer knowing you will get this letter. What had upset Jane was that her cousin, Paige, was planning to put her pony down for no reason at all except convenience. Rambo, the pony, was only 14 and he's in very good health, apparently, but Paige didn't want anyone else to ride him (he was very successful for her on the gymkhana circuit) and she couldn't be bothered looking after him any more.

God knows Paige could afford to have him agisted some-where, but she didn't want her friends to say that she was being hard-hearted, so she was planning to make up some story about him having bone cancer. No doubt she'd play the heartbroken little girl over it.

We were both disgusted—and I believe Jane intended to make it clear to Paige that if she put Rambo down Jane would make it her business to spread the true story to Paige's friends.

It's hard to believe that this could be enough to push anyone, even Paige, to [here the pen sputtered a bit, as if she'd hesitated] drastic action, but I can't think of anything else Jane was worried about, except a small issue with her having to vote her family's shares at the next AGM. She'd decided to give her proxy to William, anyway, so that had been settled.

I just can't believe Paige would hurt her cousin. She used to trail around after us when she was little. I'm sure she couldn't do anything terrible. Probably Jane's death was due to one of those mad people who put poison into medicines or spike people's drinks just for the fun of it.

No doubt I'll talk to you after I see Paige. I look forward to meeting you,

yours truly,

Melissa Hunter (Mrs)'

'A *pony*?' Tol said. 'You're kidding, right? Two people dead over a *pony*?'

It was hard to believe. But it reinforced my decision to walk away from any involvement in this.

'None of my business,' I said with determination. 'I'm calling Detective Chloe and handing it over to her.'

'Good call,' Tol said.

I rang Chloe and read the letter to her over the phone.

'You're kidding.'

'That's what it says.'

She sighed, a long suffering sigh. 'Can you get it to us?'

I was filled with the desire to be quit of the whole thing once and for all.

'I'll drop it off at Annandale Police Station,' I said.

'Fair enough.' She paused. 'There's got to be more to it than this.'

'Well, that's not my problem,' I said. 'My involvement in this is over now.'

'Don't tell anyone about the letter. Just in case.'

Halfway through our coffee Tol suddenly said, 'What if it was an accident?'

'Sorry?'

'This Paige girl, she's a clubber, right?'

'Yep.'

'So what if Jane got her drink by mistake? Vodka, speed and all?'

That made so much sense to me. An accident was so much more reasonable than killing someone over a plan to dispose of a pony.

'No,' I said, letting my forehead rest on the edge of the table. My headache was back with a vengeance. 'That would be too easy.'

Tol cleared his throat uncomfortably. Oh, no. I sat up. He had a deep and meaningful look on his face.

'My lease is up today. I have to give two weeks' notice if I want to leave.'

'Right.' I didn't know what to say. We stared at each other. I took a breath to say it. *Move in with me.* Four words. Not hard. For the first time, though, I asked myself if I *wanted* him to move in. I'd waited to be in my own little house for so long…did I want it to be *our* house? Could it be *ours*, if it only had my furniture?

Fuck yes. If that was what it took: yes.

'So,' I started, taking in a big breath.

'So I was wondering if, when I do go, if you could take my baby grand?'

'Sorry?'

'I don't want to put it in storage.'

Have I mentioned how *tiny* my house is? But Tol was looking at me with laser-focused attention, and I realised that this was a test. How serious was I about him? Was I prepared to disrupt the newly-arranged limited space in my house to accommodate his most precious possession? Saying 'I love you' is easy. *Doing* something that proves it is important.

But it wasn't only a test. It was a declaration of intent. To come back. To come back to *me*.

'Sure,' I said, my heart beating ridiculously fast. 'My dining table folds down. We can move it to under the window, and take a couple of chairs up to the second bedroom. It should just fit.'

His relieved smile made every part of me melt.

Chapter 14

Monday

Time for me to get back to my own life. Detective Chloe had all the information I had; it was her job to find out what happened. Despite my own nagging curiosity, this was none of my business. I could leave it to the professionals and enjoy the last few weeks with Tol.

And I would have, I really would have, if it weren't for the Maitland Coal Seam Gas Protest.

When I went into work on Monday, Barry tossed a thick file onto my desk, followed by a press release announcing that the Maitland Anti-Progress Association (a newly formed organisation) was sponsoring a protest march through Maitland on Wednesday to demand that the NSW Department of Minerals and Energy put a moratorium on all coal seam gas exploration licences until an appeal in the Land and Environment Court had been decided.

CSG is a divisive issue in the country. Farmers are split between those who see it as a way of keeping their heads above water and those who believe that the mining companies will suck all the water out of the water table, leaving none for agriculture. Not to mention the leakage of methane, poisoning air—and perhaps stock and people. In country towns, grocery and liquor store owners think it's a great idea. But mining developments push up rental prices to astronomical levels, and most workers are FIFO—fly in, fly out—so the town overall often doesn't get as much prosperity as it would with a different kind of development where workers brought their families to live there.

Maitland has another issue—although it started as a coal mining town, it's now part of the big wine-making and tourist trade centred around the Hunter Valley vineyards—and no one is sure how CSG mining will affect grape production.

The law, however, is drafted to allow mining to happen pretty much anywhere resources are discovered. Most people were happy with that when 'anywhere' meant the back of beyond, out in the centre or far north of the country where there were many more cows than people. And when the only communities disadvantaged were Indigenous.

But Maitland is only two hours' drive from Sydney. A favourite weekend destination. Pretty country. Somewhere you might think about retiring to. A town people *knew*. And suddenly, the whole 'what right do multinational mining companies have to invade my property?' had become a question relevant to more than First Nations people.

An organisation called 'Lock the Gate' had signed up a lot of locals—and they literally locked the gates against the mining companies, which was what had sparked the appeal to the court.

'We're sending a camera crew. Get some interviews organised with the movers and shakers,' Barry said. 'A couple of nice farmers and at least one firebrand, comment from the mining companies, you know the drill. There's a consultant in there somewhere-' he indicated the file, 'Brandon someone.'

I called the organisers of the rally and set up times and places for interviews on Wednesday morning before the march got going. Then I went through the file, cherrypicking the interesting looking characters.

'Brandon someone' turned out to be Brendan Iliadis, consulting geologist on behalf of a company called Biofuel Resources. The name appeared on two pieces of paper: one a list of witnesses at the appeal hearing, the other a page ripped out of some annual report. Iliadis' name had been circled on both.

In purple pen, just like the pen Jane had used in her address book.

I examined the annual report page. It was just a list of outgoings, the sort of thing you find in every company's audit report. Glossy paper, brown and ochre colour scheme, page number 112 picked out in white on brown. No company name. On the other side, more of the same, but nothing marked.

The outgoings were mostly the kind of thing you would expect: accountants, auditors, consultants. The question was, how did Jane get this annual report, and why did she think Iliadis' name was important?

On a hunch, I downloaded the Mancus Holdings' last annual report from their website. Sure enough, there it was: brown and ochre colour scheme. I went to page 112. Perfect match. So Mancus Holdings had been paying a consulting geologist.

So what? It was originally an agricultural company. It probably owned land in the Hunter Valley. Then I looked at how much money they'd been paying out. More than a quarter of a million over the year. Surely they couldn't hold that much land?

I opened a search window inside the annual report and typed in 'Biofuel Resources'. Page 24: a paragraph, complete with nice image of waving sugarcane, talking about how Mancus Holdings were diversifying into 'alternate fuels including biofuels', but no match on the full name. Well, I guess coal seam gas counted as an 'alternate fuel'.

Page 124: a reference to 'land acquisition on behalf of an associated company.' No details.

Biofuels Resources didn't have a website, which was weird in and of itself. The Australian Securities and Investment Commission listed it as an Australian proprietary company, limited by shares. The Australian Securities Exchange listed the company directors. Peter Mancus. Margaret Mancus. Someone called Richard O'Day. Kirk Palfrey. Now that name I knew; Kirk Palfrey was a venture capitalist who hit the front pages on a regular basis because he was a huge gambler and a big philanthropist. A contemporary of Peter Mancus, the younger brother of William—and Palfrey had also been in the photo at the Black and White Ball with Joanna Mancus.

I sat there for a moment, and then googled Brendan Iliadis, who, it turned out, had an office in Maitland. His website said he specialised in assessing seismic surveys for coal and coal seam gas developments. I rang him and introduced myself.

He was cautious.

'What does the ABC want with me?' His voice had that slight lilt of a second-generation Greek migrant, that upward tone which is so like, and yet so different from, the upward lilt of the Anglo Aussie.

'We'd just like to get a more...objective point of view. Someone who doesn't have a lot at stake personally in all this. As a consultant, you're not tied to the town, are you? Although I see that you have an office there?'

'Just temporary,' he assured me. He sounded nice. I know, no evidence. But he did. 'I'll be here for another two or three months, and then I have a contract starting up in the Surat Basin.'

The Surat Basin was in Queensland.

'Is that with Biofuels Resources too?'

'No, no, that's with Rio Tinto.'

So this guy was a big player.

'Wow,' I said, laying it on thick. 'Sounds like another story for us!'

He laughed. 'I wish. I'm just doing a predictive analysis of the life of one of their mines. Commercially sensitive, but hardly *Daily Report*-worthy.'

'And in Maitland?'

'Just analysing the potential of certain sites for clients,' he said more guardedly. 'But I'm afraid that's commercial-in-confidence.'

'Mancus Holdings,' I said airily. 'It's all in their annual report.'

There was a silence on the other end. 'Really?'

'Sure. All about you and the acquisition of land for alternative fuels.'

'Son of a bitch! And Mancus has been bleating on about confidentiality for weeks now.'

'Peter Mancus.'

'Yeah. Well, never mind. When did you want to do the interview?'

I organised time and place and hung up thoughtfully.

Barry was in the kitchenette, getting himself a coffee. I joined him and made myself a tea and reported on the interviews I'd set up.

'Good,' he said.

'I thought Jane wasn't doing hard news stories.'

'She wasn't.'

'I found some notes of hers in that file.'

'Really?' He called out to Jack. 'Was Jane working on the CSG story?'

Jack pushed back from his desk as if he were happy to be distracted.

'At the beginning, when the Lock the Gates thing started. But she was too partisan—only on the farmers' side, wouldn't hear any of the arguments on the other side. So I pulled her off it.' He turned his journalist's eye on me. 'Why?'

There was no reason not to tell them, was there? Because if this had anything to do with Jane's death, then the Daily Report people were off the hook completely.

So I laid it all out for them and let them draw their own conclusions.

'Biofuel Resources is buying up big around Maitland; Mancus Holdings is keeping it quiet,' Jack concluded.

'Okay so far,' Barry said. 'Nothing illegal. Not even unethical. Nothing worth killing for.'

'Except,' I said, 'that Jane was on the farmers' side.'

'So?' Jack asked.

'So Jane owned 50% of Mancus Holdings.'

They both stared at me in astonishment.

Rubbing his head, Barry said, 'No shit.'

'What the fuck was she doing working here?' Jack said.

'Trying to be Woodward and Bernstein, from what I've heard,' I said.

Now to understand what happened next, you have to realise that the ABC NewsCaff team has a tradition of—well, of being Woodward and Bernstein. It has brought down corrupt governments, exposed shady dealings at all levels of society, broken open crime rings which the police have been powerless to investigate. Police bribery, human trafficking, government corruption—you name it, the ABC has broken the story.

So when Barry said, 'This is a hell of a story,' and Jack said, 'Murder in high places,' as if quoting a headline, and Barry said, 'So we'll have to follow this up. Poppy, are you in?', I said: 'Yes.'

Chapter 15

Monday

So I should have told the police. Looking back, I can't believe I didn't tell the police. I think there is a kind of madness in news reporting. The desire to break the story is so strong that normal thinking is put aside.

Besides... no, there really weren't any besides. Barry just said, 'So we'll keep this to ourselves for now, right?' and I said, 'Yep,' just like Jack, Claudia and Simon, who were the other parts of the team he assigned.

Now, technically, I was on safe legal grounds. The media is legally obliged—just like everyone else—to inform police if they have evidence that a crime has been committed, or evidence which proves the identity of a criminal. But in this case, the police already knew about the crimes, we didn't have any actual proof, and all the evidence we had was on the public record. Unassailably legal. I did have a twinge of guilt about Detective Chloe, but now she knew (because of *me)* that Jane had owned so much of the company, she had the leverage to get Jane's financials and interview Mancuses. So she could come at the same information from another angle, right?

At least, that's what I told myself.

There was something I wanted to know. I cornered Jack in the kitchenette when he went in for tea.

'How did Jane take being removed from the CSG story?' I asked him.

Grimacing, he filled his mug from the boiling water tap and jiggled his teabag up and down. The scent of peppermint curled around us, surprising me. I'd tagged Jack for a caffeine junkie, like the rest of the newsroom.

'She was...disappointed.' He took a sip and tapped a finger against his mug. 'It was her first real story and she'd been very excited. I felt bad pulling her off it, but you know, we get enough accusations about bias without providing an *actual* biased story for the critics. It had to be even-handed, and she just wasn't capable of it.'

'Yeah, I gathered. But afterwards... did she talk about it at all?'

'The day after, when she gave me back the file... she did ask... if she came up with a new angle, would I run it?'

'And you said, "If it's good enough," right?' I grinned at him.

'Oh, I'm so predictable!' he grinned back. 'Of course I did.'

'What day was that?'

His gaze sharpened, and he took another sip. 'That was the Wednesday before she died.'

'Anything happen on the Thursday?'

'She took a flexi-day.'

I blinked. No one had mentioned that to me.

'The day before she died she was on flex?'

'Yeah... you think she was following up on Iliadis?'

'Maitland,' I said.

'Simon will be interviewing him on Wednesday. Find out if she talked to him.'

We went back into the office and Jack sat down in his chair. I perched on the side on his desk, mentally reviewing the route to and from Maitland.

I checked Google Maps for the route from Maitland to Dural.

'Google says to take the M1 and go via the Berowra exit,' I said. 'So she could have got to Galston Gorge on her way to Dural. But that would mean she hadn't been to see the Mancuses. She was on her way there.'

I know it was mean-spirited of me, but part of me was disappointed. Part of me *wanted* the Mancuses—preferably William, who had looked down his nose at me—to be guilty.

'Unless she was heading back to Maitland,' Jack said thoughtfully. 'We might send you up there tomorrow, McGowan. Simon's face is too well known and the place is crawling with camera crews this week. He can do the obvious interviews, and you can do the sneaky stuff. We don't want to tip off any of the other channels.'

It disturbed me how eager I was to go. Was NewsCaff getting to me after all? I hoped it was just a desire to see justice for Jane and Melissa—and me, come to that.

Tamara cornered me in the kitchenette that afternoon and she was spitting chips.

'Who the hell do you think you are?'

'Sorry?'

'You waltz in here from kiddieland and you think you can take over!' she flared. '*I* should be on this story with-' she stopped herself.

'With Simon?' I asked sweetly. Very sweetly. I was seething. All my doubts and fear and pain and anger came to a head right then and there. Who the hell did she think she was? She was only a lowly researcher, just like me. Claudia and Meri had both been there longer, and neither of them were resenting my trip to Maitland. So how obsessive did Tamara/Gladys/Karen get where Simon was concerned?

Tamara blushed, a deep, uncomfortable red which swept up from her neckline to her hair. We stared at each other and she snarled at me.

'Mind your own fucking business!'

'How did you feel when he screwed Jane?'

'He didn't!'

'Sure he did. He told me himself.'

The red receded, leaving her strangely pale. 'No,' she said. 'He wouldn't do that. She was, like, *old*.'

'His age,' I said.

'He's thirty-five!'

'So not *quite* old enough to be your father.'

'No wonder people hit you over the head,' she said. 'You're a fucking bitch.'

She turned on her heel and walked out, right out of the office, ignoring Claudia's questions and Meri's movement towards her. As she vanished down the corridor, they both turned toward me with curious faces.

I went over to them and dropped my voice, making it a girl moment.

'She didn't like that I got to go on the story with Simon...' I left a question in my voice.

They glanced at each other and shrugged. 'She's very keen on him, but he never shits where he eats,' Claudia said.

'How keen?'

'Heads over heels,' Meri admitted. 'But she's *young*.'

As though that made her harmless. I was still angry, but I was also worried. There had been real hatred in Tamara's voice. At least I'd be in the car with Simon the next day. She wouldn't want anything to happen to *him*.

———

'MATILAND?' Tol asked me that night over a late pizza. 'For how long?'

'Just the day,' I said. 'It's only two, two and a half hours' drive.'

'You'll be back late.'

'A bit.'

He took a big bite of Super Supreme and chewed thoughtfully.

'I don't see as much of you in this job,' he said.

'Two more weeks,' I reassured him. 'Then it's back to kiddieland.'

The thought was both liberating and a little bit of a downer. It wasn't that I enjoyed *The Daily Report* more than *Launchpad*; it was more the fun of working with new people, learning new things... I like learning stuff. Which was why, I reminded myself, I enjoyed making documentaries, which was basically what I did at ABCKids.

I drove up to Maitland in the crew car, with Simon and I in the back seat because the sound guy got carsick (the camera operator always seems to get the driver's seat; there's a truth about the media there). It's freeway just about all the way, and there isn't much to look at except the constant grey-green of the trees. The Australian bush is lovely close up, but it's the contrast of sea and rock and tree which gives long distant views their beauty. That road has a few of those, most notably over the Hawkesbury River, where the serrated edges of the oyster beds ruffle the water and shake gently under the wake from speed boats. It was a dull day, but still warm, and the river was steel grey from reflected clouds. I was on edge, wanting to get to Maitland and feeling unsure if I had the skills to get what we needed from Iliadis.

It was like going to your first adult party—you know, when you're around sixteen. That same mix of excitement and nervousness, although not as strong. Nothing's as strong as what you feel when you're sixteen, I thought, and then remembered Tol holding me the night before and knew that that was nonsense.

'What are you smiling at?' Simon asked. 'Had a good shag?'

'Yes, actually. An excellent one.'

He blinked at me and grinned, lasciviously. 'So tell.'

'I don't think so.'

He slid his hand across the seat until our little fingers touched.

'Come on, Poppy, you can tell me.'

I pulled my hand away.

'I don't kiss and tell,' I said. 'Unlike some people.'

Earlier in the year, Simon had done an interview with Celebrity Star Magazine about his frequent and mutually satisfactory relationships.

'That was an interview Marketing set up!' he protested.

'Mm-hmm.. how did Tamara take it?'

For a moment, he lost the fake smile and the real man showed through. He rubbed the back of his neck and sighed.

'She was pissed off with me,' he admitted. 'I think she's a bit... intense, you know?'

'Intense' was code for 'bat shit crazy'. It made me sad. I'd liked her when she was Gladys. Simon hung his lip, projecting the poor beleaguered male at full watts. Hah. Poor beleaguered flirt and lecher, more like.

'Why do you say that?'

The drone of the car changed as we went from concrete to asphalt as we passed some roadworks being done. He dropped his voice. I had to strain to hear but I resisted the impulse to lean closer; he was doing it deliberately, to try to engage me in spurious intimacy.

He still tried to fix me with his hypnotic gaze. What a jerk.

'She keeps, um, turning up...'

'Like...'

'Like when I go out for a drink with my friends, she turns up at the bar. And when I took, um, a friend of mine away for a weekend...' He looked meaningfully at me. Yes, I got it, a dirty weekend. I nodded encouragingly. 'She was at the same beach.'

'Well, that *could* be a co-incidence.'

'In *Queensland?* On *Hamilton Island?*'

'Whoa,' I said, impressed. Flying 2000 kilometres by plane and helicopter for a weekend was way unlikely to be a coincidence. Tamara was weirder than I thought. Much more 'intense'.

'Exactly.' Having made his point, Simon sat back and nodded in satisfaction.

What the hell. I might as well ask.

'So do you think she killed Jane?'

Just this once, Simon looked absolutely honest. A bit green around the gills, actually.

'I don't know.'

I left it there. I was pretty sure Simon hadn't killed anyone. Why should he? Having Jane pine over him just fed his ego. Tamara, on the other hand... but the only way to find out who killed Jane was to trace her movements.

From, perhaps, Maitland.

———

MAITLAND IS A NICE LITTLE PLACE.

It shows its history as a coal mining town in the number of pubs and the little miners' cottages, but it's been gentrified since then. Only half an hour from Newcastle, a big regional city with great beaches, Maitland always seems to me to be not quite —not quite a Newcastle suburb, not quite a trendy Hunter Valley tourist town, not quite a simple agricultural country village, not quite a mining town.

That might change, if the CSG scheme got going. It might return to its roots as a mining hub, and I was sure there were lots of people in the community who thought that was a great idea.

I'd set up an interview with one of them, Tommy Chen from the Chamber of Commerce. Simon and the crew went off to do that while I did the preliminary chat with Brendan Iliadis.

Iliadis had a small office in a walk-through arcade which was fronted on the street by a shoe store and a noodle place which smelled fantastic as I walked by. My stomach rumbled and I debated stopping for a quick dim sim, but I resisted.

The office was bland central, but not unpleasant. A small reception area, unstaffed, everything tastefully cream and pale green, two doors behind it, a sign on the desk which said, 'Please ring the bell if desk is unattended.'

I rang the bell. Both doors opened and two heads popped out, one from each: a man and a woman, surprisingly alike, in their forties, with dark hair and eyes and fine, jutting noses.

I addressed the man. 'Mr Iliadis? I'm Poppy McGowan from the Daily Report.'

'It's *Doctor* Iliadis,' the woman corrected me sharply, coming out fully from behind the door.

'Never mind that, Roula,' Iliadis said. 'It doesn't matter.'

'A PhD *does* matter, Brendan. People treat you at your own valuation!' It was obviously something he'd heard many times before, because he winced and smiled apologetically at me.

'My big sister tells me that, too,' I said.

Roula looked me up and down and nodded, obviously agreeing with Theresa's opinion of me. 'You should listen to her,' she said, and went back into her office, closing the door behind her with a snap.

Brendan and I looked at each other and burst out laughing.

'You the youngest?' I asked.

'Yeah. You too?'

'Yep. Doesn't matter how old you get, they just don't believe you're an adult.'

'Tell me about it. She's a great office manager, *but-*'

He waved me through to his office, a standard desk/filing cabinets/visitor's chair set up. The only individual note was a miner's helmet on the floor by the desk, next to a pair of muddy work boots.

We sat down.

'So, before we begin,' I said, my stomach in knots. 'I just wanted to check if Jane Mancus had been in touch with you—whether she'd organised to interview you too. I took over Jane's job at the ABC after she... had her accident. I don't want to go over old ground with you...'

He looked surprised. 'Jane Mancus worked for the *ABC*? Why didn't she say?' Then his memory caught up with his surprise and his face blanched. 'Oh, shit.'

'You reported to her, didn't you? You told her exactly what you were doing here, thinking she was one of your bosses.'

'Well, sure...she was a *Mancus*. She even showed me her driver's license... She owns 50% of the company! Of course I told her everything.'

'Owned,' I said. 'She's dead. She died on her way home from seeing you, we think. Last Wednesday. A car accident.'

That really shook him. 'Yes. Yes. I saw her on the Wednesday morning.' I felt something like shame. Was I becoming like Tyler—so inured to sudden death that I didn't react as I should to it anymore? But I had to stick to the point.

'And you told her that you were surveying farming land to set up fracking for Biofuels—which she, ultimately, owned 50% of?'

He nodded, still dazed, but then his gaze sharpened on me. 'She already knew about that—the same way *you* seem to know.'

'I had her notes,' I said.

'She wasn't that keen on fracking, I could tell, but I told her how it worked and what the environmental consequences would be...'

'The truth?'

He sat up at that, his brows twitching together in a quick frown. 'I always tell the truth about fracking. And the truth is, we don't know. We don't know *exactly* what the consequences will be. We're reasonably sure that they won't be bad, but we can't guarantee it.' Pausing, he lifted his gaze to the wall behind my head. 'You know, she seemed quite pleased about that.'

Yes. Jane would have been pleased to have a good, solid, technical reason to shut down the whole project.

'If Biofuels pulled out now... if Mancus Holdings cut their losses in the Hunter Valley—what kind of losses are we talking about?'

'Oh, millions,' Iliadis said. 'At the very least. The land purchases alone...' He caught his breath. 'And that's off the record.'

'Too late,' I said. 'But you won't hear about it on the story we're doing today, don't worry. Simon will be over later with the film crew and he'll just ask you a couple of Dorothy Dixers. Just say what you've said to me about the consequences, and you'll be fine.'

I got up to go, and hesitated. 'You didn't offer Jane a drink, did you?'

'No,' he said, rising to his feet. 'I offered her coffee, but she had an energy drink with her. She said she preferred it.'

'And she was... all right when she left? Not slurring her words, or dizzy, or anything?'

'No, of course not!' His voice was honestly indignant. 'I wouldn't have let her drive like that. Is... is that what caused the accident? She was drunk?'

'Drunk, drugged and murdered,' I said, watching him closely. But again, all I saw was blank surprise.

'Shit,' he said with heartfelt honesty.

'Yeah.'

On the other wall was a map of Maitland, with areas of land marked out in blue highlighter, many of them abutting each other. Iliadis turned to look at it and I realised it was a map of the Mancus land holdings in the area. He stood before it contemplatively and I snuck my phone out of my bag and took a photo of it without him noticing—I always turned my phone to silent before an interview.

Roula Iliadis came out of her office as we came into the reception area. Being a good hostess. As she'd probably done with Jane.

'Did you speak to Jane Mancus before she left?' I asked.

'I certainly did. I asked if there was anything I could do for her. She told me to get ready for some news. But we never heard anything from Biofuels.'

Brendan looked surprised to hear that.

'Because she died, Roula,' he said.

Roula crossed herself. 'Sad.' Yes, it was. She nodded at me and sat back down at the reception desk.

The possibility was there that Jane had gone to Dural to lay down the law to the family, and then left there to come back here, to wind up the Maitland operations.

'You know,' Brendan said, troubled. 'The last thing she asked me was who was paying me, which I thought was a bit odd because, you know, she's a—she *was* a Mancus. But I told her. Richard O'Day. And she just nodded, so I didn't think any more about it.'

Richard O'Day. He was the other director of Biofuels, along with the Mancuses and Kirk Palfrey.

'Can you tell me how I can get hold of Mr O'Day?'

'Oh, he'll be at the pub,' he said, as though everyone knew that. 'The Poorhouse.' It was all I needed. Confirmation that Jane planned to come back to Maitland after she'd talked to her family. That was all we needed from O'Day.

'Sure. I'll catch up with him there.' I gave him my card. 'If anything else occurs to you about that meeting with Jane...'

He shook his head. 'I get the feeling I shouldn't have talked to you this time. Don't quote me.'

Too late, mate, I thought. They really ought to run media courses in universities, to teach professional people how not to answer questions. 'Thanks very much for your time,' I said instead. 'The film crew will be over at two.'

We shook hands and he walked me to the door, past the reception desk. As if on impulse, Iliadis stopped and asked Roula, 'Did Jane seem all right to you when she left?'

'She was like a chicken with ten eggs,' she said. 'On top of the world. Feisty. She said she was going to get a drink and a counter meal.'

At the pub.

Iliadis and I looked at each other.

'So what's Richard O'Day like?' I asked.

He ran his hand through his hair. 'You'd better find that out for yourself.'

Roula looked at him with curiosity, but he went back into his office and closed the door.

'Richard likes a pretty girl,' Roula said, a note of caution in her voice. 'A bit too much.'

Well, that was a twist I hadn't expected.

'Too bad,' I said, grinning at her. 'Today he's just getting me.'

She smiled back. And I went to the pub.

Chapter 16

Monday

'The Poorhouse was actually 'The Pourhouse', which was the kind of pun Tol would have liked. It said 'Good Food Good Drinks Good Times' on its awning, and it was tiled in the classic mottled cream which most old pubs sported—the colour which best hid vomit stains.

Inside, it was a mix of craft beer hipster hangout and long-established local. It had a ridiculous steel pipe kind of scaffold thing with multiple taps, where they drew the beer. But it also had photos of old Maitland on the wall, and a standard beer garden out the back, where, after a question to the bar staff, I found Richard O'Day holding court.

He had a beer in hand, and was surrounded by a small group of men: some in jeans and tees, some in business suits, a couple in moleskins and Akubras. A cross section of Maitland, if you left the women out.

I pulled out a pen, tilted my clipboard to a jaunty angle, and approached. As one, the men turned to appraise me, but I could ignore that. Richard O'Day looked just like his pictures: a beautifully dressed and groomed bear, with eyebrows that would have met craggily in the middle if his hairdresser hadn't trimmed them back. A bear who leered at me.

'Mr O'Day? I'm Poppy McGowan, from the ABC. I spoke with your assistant earlier.'

The group melted away faster than an icecube in Hell, which was interesting in itself. None of them wanted to be publicly associated with him? O'Day smiled broadly, but the leering stopped.

'Ms McGowan.'

'The camera crew have you down for two-thirty, if that's okay. Or we can do it during the march, if you want that as the background.'

'Christ, no! And not here. Brendan Iliadis has an office we can use, in the arcade.'

'Oh, yes,' I said sunnily. 'I've already spoken to Mr Iliadis. That will be very convenient—we have him down for 2 pm.'

He didn't like that. His brows twitched together.

'We need a technical perspective,' I explained. He still didn't like it. Time to change course. 'I just wanted to give you my condolences, Mr O'Day, on Jane Mancus's death.'

Startled, he took half a step back. 'Oh. Well. Yes. I didn't know her all that well.'

'But you were in business with her! After all, she owned fifty percent of Biofuels.'

He put his beer down. A serious moment, clearly.

'I am in business with Mancus Holdings,' he said, slowly and clearly, as if I needed to take notes. I did so, like a good little researcher, and he relaxed a little. 'Jane was a shareholder of Mancus Holdings, but she was not an executive of the company.'

I looked him dead in the eye, trying to seem sympathetic. 'But if she'd wanted to put the kybosh on the CSG project, she could have. And we both know she *would* have, Mr O'Day, if she hadn't been killed.' He blinked. I followed up. 'Did you see her on that Wednesday? When she came to Maitland to find out the truth about Biofuels?'

Fear flickered in his eyes. It was one thing to run an under-the-radar sting on Maitland real estate. That was legal. But murder —the likes of Richard O'Day didn't want anything to do with murder.

'Fuck. Off the record. Yes. Yes, all right. I saw her. She came to the pub, ranting about fracking being bad for horses, of all things! But William would never have let her get away with that. He told her so! I had nothing to worry about as long as William was in charge.'

'William was here?'

'We were all here. All the directors. William, Peter, me.' But not Margaret. She was probably only listed as a director for tax purposes. And not Kirk Palfrey, who was merely the money-bags. And William was *not* a director. Not on record, anyway. 'We had an extraordinary board meeting after we spoke to Jane and William said he'd handle it. That's all I know.'

He took a breath and only then realised what he'd told me.

'I said "off the record", right?'

'Absolutely.'

'The important thing is,' he said, expanding in relief and picking up his beer, 'how much prosperity CSG will bring to the Hunter Valley.' And he was off on his sales pitch. I listened dutifully and even made some notes, then reminded him to be at Iliadis' office at two-thirty, and left.

————

WILLIAM HAD SAID he'd 'handle it', had he?

I met back up with the camera crew and gave them the skinny on the two interviews, and then we went to catch the march: crowd shots, vox pops, grabs from the organisers, signs and slogans. It was the most respectable protest mob I'd ever seen. Farmers, of every age, kids, families, people in riding gear and people in business suits.

By the end of it, we were hot, thirsty and hungry, so we all went back to The Pourhouse for a pub lunch. Half-way through an excellent beef and port pie, who should come in but William Mancus, trailed by both Richard O'Day *and* William's younger brother, Peter. So he was Jane's uncle, and the other director of Biofuels. They took a table which had been reserved for them. I eyed Peter Mancus with some curiosity.

He was not much older than Jane—forty-five, maybe—and looked fit, like he hit the gym regularly. My head ached; he certainly was solid enough to knock me down, and his face had the expression of a discontented man.

Discontented because his big brother was here, and Biofuels was supposed to be his, Peter's, baby?

His brother was listening only to Richard O'Day, although Peter tried to contribute to the conversation. It must have been humiliating, to be ignored like that. Especially after he'd been frozen out of the main company. Interesting that they were all here.

'That table over there has three out of five of the directors of Biofuel,' I told Simon. 'You should doorstop them.'

He grinned at me. 'Barry would have my guts for garters if I got Mancus offside.'

'Nonsense! You just want to make sure that their side of the dispute gets air time. You're doing him a favour.' This was true, and Simon knew William knew it, so he nodded to the camera crew and strode across to the Biofuel table, smiling. I kept my head down and my ears open, but he got nothing except what we might have expected: a panegyric about CSG and how the protestors were a small, unrepresentative group of troublemakers.

After lunch, William and O'Day disappeared, and the crew followed them to Iliadis' office.

Peter just sat there, nursing a beer and a grievance.

So I went over. Of course. As I got close, I could smell his cologne. Bergamot. Which I'd smelled when someone—when *he?*—attacked me.

I said, 'Mr Mancus?'

He looked up at me and pushed back from the table, his face going white. Guilt. It *was* him. Rage reared up in me so fast I didn't even try to control it.

'You didn't get the letter, you fucking bastard. Melissa sent it registered post, and now the police have it. The only question is, did you attack me on your own or did William tell you to do it?'

'I-I-I don't know what you're talking about.' He slid the chair further back and got up, but I was in between him and the exit. 'I've-I've never seen you before.'

I leaned in. 'We know what you did, Peter. The vodka. The speed. You were the only one who had the chance.'

He'd regained some poise. 'I don't know what you're talking about,' he said again. He pushed past me without another word. But his hands were shaking as he walked away.

Peter Mancus. Peter bloody Mancus.

I was so angry my vision turned red. My nails were cutting into my palms, my fists were so tight. I'd so wanted to just slam into him, to hurt him the way he'd hurt me.

Well. I forced myself to take a breath. There was more than one way to get revenge, especially when you could get justice as well.

————

'PETER MANCUS...' Barry said slowly after I briefed him.

'I'm gong to call the police.' I sat down heavily on Barry's visitor's chair. I was still getting headaches, and this one was a doozy. It had seemed a much longer drive coming back, and it was still only four o'clock.

'You sure?'

'She'll pull Peter in for questioning. We can get footage of him going into the Parramatta building.' The main police centre in NSW was in Parramatta, in Sydney central west.

Simon was leaning against the filing cabinet. 'That Biofuels case is coming up in the Land and Environment Court on Friday. We need to have this finalised before then. The court will want to know about this.'

'Let's put the story out tonight,' Barry said.

'We don't have enough!' Simon stood up straight. 'The defamation issues alone-'

'We'll get the lawyers to go over it. Poppy, you make the call to Prudhomme. I'll get a crew out to sit on the entrance at Parramatta. There's one out there at the District Court on a drugs-in-our-schools story for the weekend News. Simon, start writing the script: ABC researcher killed while on the hunt for nefarious doings in the mining industry. We don't have to name names. But we *can* say that she confronted the directors of Biofuels, in which she had a 50% stake, the day she was killed.'

'The inference is defamatory.'

'Hedge it. Say "met with" instead of confronted. And "at this point, no one knows how the drugs and alcohol were put in Jane Mancus's drink". But we can prove that Jane hated the idea of CSG, and that she owned 50% of a company which was going to start producing the stuff.'

'What if they didn't do it?' I asked, suddenly aware that we were about to blow apart the Mancus' world.

'Are you sure that Peter Mancus attacked you?' Barry stared at me like an inquisitor.

'Hundred percent.'

'Well then. They might not have killed Jane—although who else would have?—but we know they were involved in grievous bodily harm. And that's a felony, and the criminal should be brought to justice.'

Couldn't argue with that.

I called Detective Chloe and told her everything. 'Off the record' meant not to be broadcast. Not telling the police was a whole different thing—in fact, was conspiracy.

She listened in silence. 'You're sure he's the murderer?'

'It was definitely him who attacked me.'

'On the basis of a scent?'

'And his reaction when he saw me. Surely that's enough to get him in and question him about his movements on that night and on the Wednesday?'

A moment's silence.

'Yes. Yes, I think it is.'

'Don't forget that William was in the mix. Acting as a director of Biofuels when he *isn't* a director.'

'Hmmm. I'll get ASIC onto that side of things.' The corporate watchdog. I wouldn't hold my breath; their investigations tended to move slowly.

'He was one of the last people to see Jane alive.' Why shouldn't William Mancus be interviewed?

'Let's start with the brother. See what we get. We'll pick him up later tonight, once we've got our ducks in a row.'

She hung up, but this time I didn't mind. Mr Peter Bloody Mancus wouldn't like Chloe questioning him. Not at all. And just for once, I hoped Martin put the boot in.

'Good girl,' Barry said. 'Now, let's get this story going. If they're picking him up late tonight, it's airing tomorrow.' He paused. 'Poppy, you look like shit. Go home.'

What a wonderful idea. I went home and had a nap.

———

THAT EVENING, Tol was suitably incensed about Peter Mancus. I think he'd quite like to have tried a little home-brewed revenge himself.

My headache seeped away in his hug.

'So. He killed Jane, then?' he said into my hair.

I wasn't so sure about that.

I pulled away from him and sat on the couch; he sat next to me and held my hand.

'Maybe. But there's something off about William going to Maitland. He just doesn't get involved at the ground level. That's for the troops. He's the general.'

Pursing his lips, Tol nodded. 'But this was a family matter...'

'Exactly. Something he'd want to handle himself.'

'Where would someone like William get speed, though?'

That was a good question. The obvious answer was from Paige. But that would make it very, very pre-meditated.

I really needed to talk to Paige.

I checked her Facebook page. Tonight she was going to a charity thing on Bondi Beach. The Olympic beach volleyball team taking on all comers for their No Limits Foundation. No doubt finishing off with rock lobsters from Tasmania for the VIP donors.

But *anyone* could go to Bondi.

Chapter 17

Monday

I am not a fan of public spaces being cordoned off for private events. I guess it's not so bad when it's for charity, but generally I think the people who pay for the place (i.e. the taxpayers/rate payers) should have unfettered access.

Tol listened patiently to me grumbling about half the beach and half the foreshore being roped off as he negotiated the small hell of finding parking at Bondi Beach.

It was a swanky affair, all right. A marquee had been set up on the pavement above the beach's volleyball court, and a match was underway. The ropes keeping the *hoi polloi* out were red velvet, the bollards shiny chrome, the security guys gold-standard Pacific Islanders, buff and huge.

But I have magic: my ABC staff card. Charities want as much publicity as they can get, and I could easily push off a small story for the *Daily Report*'s online page. I'd already done three of them this week for stories which weren't big enough for the show.

Conveniently Tol had a professional-looking camera he used on digs, so there we were, being ushered through the red velvet rope while others craned their necks to see the match being played.

Inside the ropes, the dressing was weirdly formal for a beach-side do; clearly none of the women in their high heels or the men in their hand-stitched brogues intended to actually set foot on the beach.

Bingo! There was Paige, with her grandmother. I was pleased with myself for putting on a pantsuit instead of my normal jeans and a top. In fact, the whole family was there: Paige and Joanna, William and Margaret, Peter and whatever-her-name was. Samantha! That was it. Paige's mother. The gambler. Maybe Peter had an urgent reason for wanting the CSG to succeed, if she was punting away his profits on everything else.

They were standing next to a display of the work the No Limits Foundation did: scholarships for 'worthy recipients', mainly. I guess that went with the whole 'Deserving Poor' attitude we no longer spoke openly about.

Before I approached them, I turned away and called Barry. No reason for him not to get a tick of approval from the funding boss.

'Hey, Barry, I'm at Bondi and William Mancus is here with his family, doing a charity event for their foundation. You want me to do a story for online about it? Say the idea came from you? I could get pictures we could use for the main story.'

'Good thinking, McGowan. Do it.'

So there I was, armed with probity and smarm. I went up to William first, and waited until he'd stopped talking to a potential donor. He was quite animated when he talked about the Foundation; the most human I'd seen him. When the man moved away, I approached.

'Mr Mancus?'

He turned with a smile which switched to a slightly puzzled frown. He knew he'd seen me, but he couldn't place me, and I wasn't well-dressed enough to be a donor.

'Poppy McGowan, from the *Daily Report*. Barry thought we could do an online story about the event. Help things along.'

His face cleared. Now I was slotted into the 'helpful media contact' pigeonhole, and he was gracious.

'Excellent. How can I help you?'

'Perhaps a photo of the whole family?'

Out of the corner of my eye, I saw Joanna smile cynically, but she didn't warn William that I was a troublemaker. There was a definite 'let the chips fall where they may' attitude in that smile.

William marshalled the six of them into a classic family pose, with him right at the centre. He firmly took a martini glass out of Paige's hand and put it out of sight.

Tol dutifully took a few shots, while I slid into position just out of shot, next to Paige.

'It would be great for our younger readers to get your view on things, Ms Mancus,' I said, phone ready to record.

'Oh!' She glanced at William, who nodded, so she smiled at me. 'Sure. Why not?'

I spent a dull couple of minutes getting the company line from Paige. Time to ask the real questions.

'I was sorry to hear your pony was ailing.'

'Oh no!' she said brightly, with not a flicker of shame or panic on her face. 'I've found a wonderful young rider to take him on now I can't give him enough time. I'm so busy with the charity, you know. Melissa Hunter helped find her.'

What?

'Yes, Poppy,' Joanna said, too sweetly, 'Perhaps you should talk to Melissa—she's going to also help us find worthy rural scholarship recipients.'

I spun around to look at Joanna in disbelief. She nodded to behind Tol.

And there stood Melissa Hunter, talking to Samantha Mancus.

Chapter 18

Monday

Tol and I exchanged looks which were a mixture of relief and what the hell?

'Melissa!' I said, but of course she didn't know who I was. I went towards them, holding out my hand. I think I just wanted to make sure she was real. She *looked* like her pictures...

Automatically, she took my hand.

'Poppy McGowan,' I said.

Her face lights up. 'Oh, I'm so glad to meet you!'

'We've been worried about you.' I kept it calm, but inside I wanted to shout *Where the hell have you been?*

She shook my hand and dropped it. 'I'm *so* sorry! There was a mix-up in communications. Samantha whisked me away for a break on their island in the Whitsundays. Angela was supposed to tell my husband, but apparently that message never arrived?'

There was a faint note of disbelief in her voice, and I shared it. Angela had struck me as a very capable woman. There was no way she'd have let the search for Melissa go on more than a second if she'd had that information.

Tol was taking photos unobtrusively, of Melissa, Samantha, and the display.

'But you had your phone?'

She glanced at Samantha and turned a bit red. Anger? Or shared embarrassment?

Samantha cut in. 'I was *such* a fool! I dropped it overboard in the launch on our way out to the seaplane.'

'Sam was taking a photo of me in the launch to send to Tim,' Melissa said. Maybe my face showed that I wasn't buying that, because suspicion dawned in her own eyes. 'She did say that she'd text Tim for me...'

'I just forgot! Silly me.'

Samantha Mancus had the eyes of a great white shark. Silly was not the word.

'Sure. So, what else happened last week in the Mancus family?'

Because that had to be the answer. Melissa had been got out of the way and out of contact for a week. Despite my over-whelming relief that she was alive, it stank to high heaven.

'Not much,' Samantha said, eyes cold, mouth smiling

Paige had joined the conversation and, like so many teenagers, couldn't resist the temptation to contradict her mother.

'Oh, no, Mum! There was the AGM and the vote on the fracking. That was pretty fucking important.'

'Paige! Language!' Joanna's voice came from behind her. Paige turned and grinned, unrepentant.

'Sorry, Grandma.' They smiled at each other with real affection.

Fracking. CSG.

'Did the vote go through, Mrs Mancus?'

'It did indeed.' Joanna's face wouldn't show anything she didn't want it to, and right now she wanted it to show calm approval. What she actually thought, I'd never know.

I still couldn't believe Melissa had just gone along with Samantha. 'Your husband was very worried.'

That struck home. 'Poor darling Tim! He's arriving tonight. In fact...' She looked at her watch. 'I'd better be going if I want to be there when he lands. So nice to meet you, Poppy.'

And she was gone. Samantha Mancus and I stared at each other for a moment. Natural enemies. It happens sometimes like that. Her husband Peter slid in beside her and put an arm around her waist. The perfect power couple. I shook with hatred of someone who could let poor Tim Hunter believe his wife was dead for a *week* over a business deal. Monsters.

But...did that make them murderers, too?

'I was so sorry about Jane, Mr Mancus,' I said. He blinked. I had the definite feeling that, in his world, Jane was long gone and not missed.

'Thank you.' Samantha answered for him, cool and collected. I wasn't going to get anything out of them, so I nodded and moved away. Besides, Detective Chloe would probably turn up soon, and I could enjoy watching her haul Peter away.

But first, Paige.

There was still one thing I wanted to know. *Needed* to know. And possibly Paige would tell me. None of the others would. I spent a few minutes actually doing my job, recording short grabs with donors about the charity, and helping Tol get some footage of the volleyball match. It was a pretty good camera.

The Mancuses dispersed, doing their rounds as befitted the main sponsors of the charity. I waited until Paige was talking to some girls her own age, laughing loudly.

'She snuck off a few minutes ago,' Tol told me in a whisper. 'I think she's high.'

Excellent.

'Paige!' I made it sound like we were best friends, and the other girls tightened their circle so I wouldn't intrude, leaving Paige on the out. 'I'm so sorry—I should have given my condolences to you about your cousin Jane. You know I'm working at the *Daily Report*. They miss her there.' Well, they felt that they *should* miss her, anyway.

Her eyes filled with tears. The first time any of them had shown real grief.

'Poor Jane! She was so *nice*. She was the one who made me find another rider for Rambo.' Rambo the pony. Right. 'And then she went and...' Tears trickled out.

'So you saw her just before?' I tried to be delicate, but it wasn't a delicate question.

'*Just* before! Like, fifteen minutes before she left the house. I didn't even get the chance to say goodbye!' Yes, that was genuine grief. I patted her on the back and offered a tissue, which she grabbed thankfully, blotting the tears up carefully so her mascara wouldn't run. 'It was such a shit of a day. Dad had found-' But there, she stopped, gulping back whatever she'd been about to say. I had my suspicions, though.

I sighed, heavily. 'Fathers are so strict. I mean, a little help to feel happy, what's the harm?'

'Right? I mean, RIGHT????' You could hear the multiple question marks. 'So I do a little speed now and then. It's not like it's *meth*.'

'And it helps you stay slim.'

'ExACTly. But no, he's all "this stuff will kill you" and he took it *all*. Such a downer. And then, Jane...'

'I'm so sorry,' I said. 'At least you parted on good terms. Unlike her and your father.'

'Well, *no one's* on good terms with Dad if they don't like fracking. He thinks it's the fucking Mona Lisa, like *no one* can criticise it. He was *so* rude to my friend Brittany when she said it was bad for the water table and, like, she's a member of *Greenpeace*, so she'd know, right?'

On cue, someone I suspected was Brittany came up and detached her from me gently. 'Come on, Paige. Come down to the beach.'

And that was that.

I collected Tol, and was about to leave when I thought, *Fuck it.* I towed him back to Joanna Mancus. And score! Angela was there, getting her into a coat. Two for one.

No preamble and no politeness. I spoke directly to Angela. 'If you knew that Peter put the vodka and speed into Jane's drink, and covered it up, you're an accessory to murder. Detective Prudhomme will be speaking to you soon, and my advice—my very *strong* advice—is that you tell the truth.'

Angela's warm olive complexion turned pasty. 'I-'

Joanna cut across her. 'Be careful, Ms McGowan.'

I glared at her. 'Be *careful*? Your granddaughter is *dead*, Mrs Mancus. Murdered. It's way past time for caution.'

She blanched and lost her balance. Maybe she'd never admitted it to herself before.

'You *knew*,' I accused her.

'You had to know,' Tol said, but to Angela. She saw something in his face which gave her strength, because she stepped away from Joanna.

'Yes.' That slight trace of an accent had grown. 'Mrs Mancus realised...we tried to stop her! I rang, I *told* her to stop driving, but she wouldn't listen! I begged her to pull off the road before the bridge, but she just laughed.'

'She was...inebriated.' Joanna clasped her hands together, rings winking.

'She was poisoned,' I said. 'Off her face with vodka and speed. Speed which your son had confiscated from his daughter that morning.'

'Peter?' Her voice was high. '*Peter* did this?'

Oh, Lord. She'd been protecting Paige.

'Peter. Probably helped by that barracuda of a wife. But yes. Peter, not Paige.'

She wobbled, suddenly just an old lady. Angela rushed to get her a chair, and she sat shakily.

'Why did you think it was Paige?'

'He *said*. Peter *said*. "Jane's gone off with half of Paige's drugs in her. Stupid girl." I thought...I just *assumed*...'

That bastard. Tol's hands were tight on the camera.

'Threw his own daughter under the bus,' Angela said. 'I'm not protecting *him*.'

Joanna's face hardened. She'd turned back into the family matriarch. 'Call your detective, Miss McGowan. There are some things which cannot be forgiven.'

Chapter 19

Monday night

'What I *hate*,' I said to Tol as we drove home after yet another horrible evening at Police Headquarters, 'is that killing Jane was forgivable if Paige did it, but blaming Paige wasn't.'

'Grandma's favourite.'

Poor, unloved Jane. God, I had a headache. The place where that bastard Peter had hit me throbbed. I scuffled in the glove box for paracetamol and swallowed them down with Tol's ever-present car waterbottle.

Peter Mancus had denied everything, but Chloe had arrested him anyway. And Samantha, as an accessory.

Apparently, once Martin caught up with Melissa Hunter, it emerged that she'd been chattering to Samantha and Paige over the lunch where she'd sold Paige on the idea of giving Rambo to this girl Melissa knew. And just in passing, she'd mentioned that she knew all about Jane's intention to vote 'No' at the AGM. The problem was, Jane's estate hadn't been settled, so Melissa, who was her executor, had the right to vote on her behalf at the AGM. She would have voted no, fulfilling Jane's wishes.

So Melissa had to be got out of the way until the AGM was over, with Joanna, as her heir, casting Jane's vote without anyone to argue against it. Stupid of them to make it look like a disappearance, but they probably wanted to stop Melissa hearing about the AGM—and they would have had to inform Jane's solicitors about it.

The best thing about that was that the vote was illegal, and wouldn't stand. Melissa would make sure of that.

'I certainly *will* make sure of it!' she'd told me before we left Headquarters. Tim, her husband, nodded.

'And we'll see if we can make a case against Samantha and Peter Mancus,' he said grimly. 'A civil case, if the police won't prosecute a kidnapping.'

Excellent.

We parted on the best of terms, with an invitation to visit them in Amaroo any time I wanted.

It was all done. But, of course, it *wasn't* done, because the great news shark had to be fed.

I'd kept Barry and Tyler up to date on everything as it happened, and they'd hurried to get segments to air before Peter was arrested and it became sub judice—once someone is arrested, what the media can say about the case is strictly controlled so you don't bias the jury pool or interfere in the course of justice.

Enough interfering in the course of justice for me. I was over this whole poking at murderers thing.

Tol felt the same. We went home and sent the photos of the Mancus family to Tyler, including a perfect one of Samantha and Peter looking grim and rather horrible.

'Nice,' I said as I emailed it off.

'I'm a man of many talents.' He grinned at me and started massaging my neck and shoulders. Oh, that felt good.

'When do you get your helicopter ride?' he asked.

'I've booked it for the day after you leave. To cheer me up.'

His hands stilled, and then went on. 'We'll see each other in February.'

That was true. The dig was still happening, and I was still going. That made me feel better. I sighed.

'Time for bed?'

'It certainly is,' I agreed. We went up the stairs together. I stopped at the top and put my arms around his waist, leaning back until I could see him properly in the dim light. Took a deep breath and stepped off the cliff. 'I can tell my family you're moving in.'

He kissed my forehead, gently. 'No. That can wait. It's only a couple of months until I leave, anyway.'

A mixture of relief and angst went through me. I wanted to say, 'Don't go!' but I couldn't. This was the next step in his career. It would be selfish of me to stand in the way.

I kissed him, slowly and with promise. 'We'd better make the most of the time we have, then.'

So we did.

———

I HOPE you've enjoyed my first Poppy McGowan novella. I had a lot of fun writing it!

If you want to be kept up to date about new Poppy books (like the book set in Jordan, which is coming next year), sign up for my newsletter at https://pamela-hart.com/novella/.

As a special treat for readers of *Fatal Crossing*, when you sign up you'll get the 'very truly really' scene from Tol's point of view, written by the inspiration for Tol, my husband Stephen. (Yes, he's an archaeologist and a pianist and so many other things no one would believe the character if I put them all in. Honestly, he's even nicer than Tol and I'm a very lucky woman. Also, he's a writer, which is really convenient for projects like this.) You'll also get a Poppy short story (written by me).

If you've enjoyed *Fatal Crossing*, please leave a review on Amazon and/or Goodreads. This is my first venture into self-publishing, and nothing is more important than reviews! If you have friends who've enjoyed *Digging Up Dirt* or *An A-List for Death*, please let them know about *Fatal Crossing*.

Many thanks to Stephen and my friend and gracious editor, Margaret Morgan.